The Secrets of the Universe

- ◆ Learn to cultivate your own garden.
- ◆ The kingdom of heaven is within.
- ◆ Everything in the universe is exactly as it should be.
- ◆ It's never too late to have a happy childhood.
- ◆ Wherever I go, there I am!
- ◆ Keep it simple.
- ◆ These are the good old days.
- ◆ You are perfect.

There Is No Way to Happiness: Happiness Is the Way!

"This is the message of all my gifts. If you haven't figured out this secret, happiness will always elude you," Eykis said.

"Remember, you all have such an advantage here on Earth: Your reality permits you to live in total harmony with your world . . . Why not take these gifts, apply them, and just attempt to experience a new reality?"

GIFTS FROM EYKIS

DR. WAYNE DYER

Books by Dr. Wayne Dyer

The Sky's the Limit
Gifts from Eykis

Published by POCKET BOOKS

DR. WAYNE DYER
GIFTS FROM EYKIS

POCKET BOOKS
New York   London   Toronto   Sydney   Tokyo   Singapore

POCKET BOOKS, a division of Simon & Schuster Inc.
1230 Avenue of the Americas, New York, NY 10020

Copyright © 1983 by Wayne Dyer

ISBN: 0-671-68461-2

First Pocket Books printing March 1984

17 16 15 14 13

POCKET and colophon are registered trademarks of
Simon & Schuster Inc.

Printed in the U.S.A.

To the *promise* of Eykis: a miracle for our time!
and
To the memory of John Lennon,
who asked us to "imagine"
that the world could be as one

CONTENTS

ACKNOWLEDGMENTS

Grateful acknowledgment is expressed to Michael Korda and John Herman of Simon and Schuster for their brilliant editing; to Arthur Pine and Richard Pine for their encouragement and belief in this project; and especially to Susan Elizabeth Dyer for her masterly creative input in all phases of the production of this, my first effort at writing fiction.

Reality is not a concept; reality is my daily life.
                                    —J. Krishnamurti

INTRODUCTION

Throughout history storytelling has been a significant avenue of communication. From *Aesop's Fables* and biblical parables to *Jonathan Livingston Seagull* and many additional ancient and modern sources, we can learn readily by stepping aside to the position of objective observer. There the sting of criticism is not so painful. The action and resulting consequences happened to the fox or bird or prodigal son. Yet with very little effort we see how the truth and universal essence belong to us all. We are moved to new perceptions, emotions, and behavior through these "fictional" examples.

Science and technology have brought us forward into a grand new world with greater possibilities than ever. But in many ways our attitudes and feelings have not evolved equally. We are less equipped to deal with the opportunities presented today because we drag along some unhelpful beliefs and misperceptions of the realities of our world.

What would be the reactions of an intelligent visitor from another planet to our complex systems here on Earth? How would we view that visitor's culture? Can we compare favorably? Are we ready to accept an objective view? *Gifts from Eykis* is an example of one exchange encounter between an Earthling and a citizen from Uranus. Both are peaceful, open, life-loving people who seek to enhance the well-being of all. Through them I have been able to observe where we are in our societies and speculate on where we might go should we choose the realities recommended. The parable format may enable more people to slip into the role of observer, but ultimately we all must look inward and see ourselves.

As you will discover, Eykis lives. Long live Eykis!

WAYNE W. DYER

PROLOGUE

The library had been designated as the place to which rented academic caps and gowns were to be returned. I stood among the stacks full of leather and paper, the traditional symbols of wisdom, my hood of doctoral rank askew about my shoulders like a limp noose, the rolled parchment certifying my professional qualifications tucked under my elbow as I held a copy of an essay by Bertrand Russell. It was about "happiness" —something which I had searched for and never found among or between the lines of the seemingly endless texts I had read on my way to this day.

Behind me someone approached. I heard the quiet shuffling and knew who it was. There were those at the university who called him eccentric; others, less kind, called him "senile." But in the worldwide community of scientists, particularly physicists, he was still recognized as a giant. His feet shuffled slowly but his brain leaped and soared, occasionally to places no one else could dream of, let alone follow.

I turned and smiled a genuinely respectful welcome. "Good afternoon," I said.

"Indeed, yes. And I have a Gift for you." The professor's English was sprinkled with more capitals than most of us used. He handed me a bundle of mathematical equations which I did not recognize.

"Long ago, in my early days of Experimentation, I had an Assistant. He would not allow Acknowledgment, for he said that as a Visitor, his presence might be a Disruption. Actually, he deserved the greater Credit, but he explained the Responsibility was mine, and so should be all of the Results."

"You've never mentioned him before that I can remember."

"No. No. Nor shall I ever again. But he left me the *Urantian Formulas*. I've tried to understand them, but I have only a glimmer. He said there would come a Willing Learner to take up the Journey. This was forty years ago. I've looked and waited." He sighed. "You are the One." A small smile began to move across the wrinkled face and glowed in triumph finally in his eyes.

"Me? What did you say this is?" I asked incredulously.

"The *Urantian Formulas*. It has to do with Molecular Transport. My journey is nearly done, but yours begins Here," he said, tapping the typed pages. "*Bon voyage*, Learner. Perhaps one day—the Teacher."

He smiled again, gently, and turned to shuffle quietly away.

"Thank you for the Gift," I called, still puzzled. Without pausing, he waved a slow farewell salute and was soon out of sight beyond the next library stack.

• Part One •

URANUS

1 · The Arrival

It was difficult to believe. This place called Uranus *appeared* to be an exact replica of Earth. After years of decoding the *Urantian Formulas,* I had made my first successful self-transport to another planet, and as luck would have it, I landed in a place that appeared to duplicate home. From all outward appearances, everything on Uranus was precisely as it was back on Earth.

I had assumed that even though I would remain within my own solar system, I would have an opportunity to see something new, something genuinely *different,* if I traveled to a very distant planet. I thought that Uranus would be far enough from Earth for me to experience a whole new reality—creatures made of gases who changed shape, or at any rate something to equal the vivid imagination of the *Star Trek* writers whose work I admired so much. I had pictured myself moving about in time warps, leaping forward or backward millions of years by some magical ability to transcend my body. The years of anticipation and hard work had not prepared me for this shock: there seemed to be no difference at all!

Authors and researchers who considered the possibility of a duplicate planet usually imagined mirror images, reversals of good and evil and the like. However, never, even in my most fanciful moments, had I expected to find a *literal* sister planet, a place that exactly duplicated Earth. It was almost as if the residents of Uranus had undertaken to deliberately reproduce our world, step by step in every single aspect. Their great oceans, mountain ranges, and deserts were in exact proportion to those of Earth. They even had identical names. There was not only a Sahara Desert, there was even a Sahara *Hotel*. I suspected they had observed us with a very powerful telescope, and faithfully reconstructed Earth on Uranus. Certainly they had every detail right. Traffic jams took place at five o'clock in the afternoon in all the major cities, there was starvation in the "Third World," there were huge shopping centers and fuel-efficient small cars imported from "Japan." They hadn't missed a thing.

I was beginning to think I had been hoodwinked. Perhaps I had been tricked into believing that I was the first Earthling to visit another planet and in fact I had never even left home. Perhaps my secret research on the Formulas had been penetrated, and I was going to be used as propaganda bait to fool the Soviets— allowing the enemy to think we had achieved some technological breakthrough that did not really exist. I thought I'd seen a movie about this at one time. But somehow I knew better. I had *felt* the impact of molecular transport. I had *experienced* myself hurtling away from Earth through the void of space. I was sure, but the doubt lingered. It struck me that the only way to verify that I was truly on Uranus was to stop looking at the external images, and to see if in fact the people themselves were also duplicate Earthlings. From all outward appearances they *seemed* to be.

I decided to select one of these Uranus people to interview in depth; if he or she turned out to be exactly like all the Earthlings I'd met, I would return home immediately and develop the ability for travel *beyond* our solar system. I hadn't come billions of miles simply to see my own world. I had begun this project with a desire for adventure and excitement. The prospect of fitting myself into a new world of people identical to those I had left behind was not particularly exciting.

I settled into my room at one of Uranus' finest Holiday Inns, flipped on the television, and began to ponder how I could learn about the inhabitants of this world that was at one and the same time alien and familiar to me. The irony of my predicament did not escape me. I was in a strange land, and yet I felt as if I'd never left home. Even this hotel room was like those I had seen a thousand times before—miniature soap bars, a tiny ounce of shampoo in a brown plastic bottle, a kind of soiled cleanliness to the bedspread, and an unread copy of the Gideon Bible in the dresser drawer.

My mind was filled with questions, and yet I found myself struggling with the "How-to-go-about-it" thinking that I often employed to avoid taking any action. I had learned a long time ago that the way to make sure that something got done was to start it. But I'd also learned how to combat that notion, which required effort, sweat, and all those qualities I loved to observe in others and to eschew in myself. Instead of taking charge, I used my predicament to keep my mind focused on what I should or shouldn't do. I moved to a more advanced form of evasiveness. I considered the questions I would want to ask. Do you have wars? Are you preoccupied with rules? What about cancer, and how do you see this mystery we call death? Do you have schools and do they emphasize grades and obedience? Do you wear designer jeans, and if so, why? Do you have the same history as we do on Earth? Do you know about us? Will you ever visit, and if you did, would you be friendly? Do you have nuclear weapons and a Jane Fonda? Are you really the same identical creatures as we are inside as well as outside? Do you have emotions, fears, anxiety, and tranquilizers? The questions were bombarding my consciousness almost as fast as I could record them on my miniature portable tape recorder. (Could I re-place the batteries here? I wondered.)

As I said these words to myself into the tape re-corder, the word "anxiety" was repeated in the room. I couldn't believe it. Until then I had been ignoring the television reporter, who looked exactly like all those I'd seen across America. The Aryan model with "television good looks," who could have slid into the vacant seat of any local television newscaster in Se-attle, Minneapolis, Atlanta, or Toronto without any-one knowing the difference, had been reading his lines

so vacuously that I had tuned him out while i pon
dered the enormity of the task that lay ahead. But just
when I was saying into the tape recorder, "Do you
have emotions, fears, anxiety, and tranquilizers?" I
heard the first words on the newscast that made me
realize that everything on Uranus was not exactly as
it was on Earth. It was almost as if I had been slapped
in the face.

Segueing into the next segment, before goi   into a
commercial, Mr. Aryan Good Looks had said, 'That
concludes the national news, stay tuned for the local
stories, to be followed by sports, weather, and the
anxiety attack reports."

I had half listened to the national news, which, pep-
pered with empty phrases like "leading economic in-
dicators," "student protest demonstrations," and
"presidential study commissions," sounded much the
same as on Earth. The local news, weather, and even
Joe Jock sports reports were also familiar, and I now
listened to the chronology of useless, dreary information with unabated ennui, as I waited to hear he one
facet of the evening report that would give me my first
clue to these people on Uranus who had built   ulture
which, until now, seemed just like mine.

"Stay tuned, after this report from a light beer, foi
tomorrow's anxiety attack report."

An anxiety attack report on the newscast! I felt a
flurry of excitement. What the hell was an anxiety
attack report, and what was it doing as a regular fea-
ture on the evening news?

The report was brief and to the point.

"Hello, this is Eykis, with your evening anxiety at-

tack report. Chances of anxiety attacking are high in
the upper altitudes, with a diminished possibility
within the city limits. There is an 80 percent chance of
anxiety on Friday, with a decreased likelihood on the
weekend. By Monday the forecast is for almost zero
anxiety, even in the upper ranges 6,000 feet above sea
level. However, tonight's anxiety attack risk is exceedingly high, so I would urge each of you to check
your stock of preventive medicine right away. You
probably won't need it over the weekend, but by mid-
week the likelihood of a new anxiety front moving into
the area is exceedingly high. This is Eykis, signing off.
This report has been brought to you by Nopain, the
only product of its kind containing 850 milligrams of
anxiety prevention, to help you when you need it most
—that is, when an unexpected anxiety attack appears
out of nowhere. Remember: You get the most value
from Nopain when anxiety is attacking."

I sat there in shock. An anxiety attack report on the
evening news! This was something I would never have
imagined even in my craziest moments. Fortunately,
I had had the presence of mind to tape the report as it
came through the television. I put my tape recorder
into rewind and played the report again, and again. On
the third replay, I timed the message. The report had
lasted one minute. I listened to it over and over thinking that probably it was a joke. Perhaps this Eykis
person was an evening news satirist, similar to characters on our newscasts who posed as social critics
and made fools of themselves, shouting into the cam-
era with phony anger at some politician or social evil
that they found particularly offensive. You knew that

if they really believed in what they said, they would be doing something actively about what they pretended to dislike instead of shouting aimlessly at their enemies over the airwaves. I have always felt that by taking refuge in what others are or are not doing properly, critics show that they themselves are not doers.

Eykis was nothing like that. She was direct, she appeared to be serious, and she communicated personal concern about her anxiety attack report. The signal she sent me was very special; I simply couldn't believe that it was a put-on. Nonetheless I decided to tune to the next newscast and see if what I had watched was a trick or the real thing. Sure enough, thirty minutes later on a competing network program, another anxiety attack report was featured, with almost identical warnings to the populace.

I made the decision right there that I was going to seek out this Eykis person whose sincerity had touched me so deeply. I needed a sensitive Uranus resident whom I could trust with my own identity. Something deep within me said, "This is the person. She is committed to helping and she speaks the truth in clear, simple terms." I was certain about her because I was already obsessed. Somewhere in the core of my being I always know when someone is right and in this case I knew it instantly. Long ago I had trained myself to ignore the rules under which most Earthlings operate, and to consult only my inner voices. If anyone urged me to act, feel, or think in a specific way, I simply ignored all of the "I don't know if I shoulds," and listened to my inner voice. Early in my life I'd learned that the only thing I ever regretted was what I failed to do out of some self-inflicted fear or prohibition originating in the rules of others. To be sure, I did many things which I disliked or which turned out wrong, but I never felt any painful regret for what I did. I simply vowed to avoid repeating such behavior. Consequently, I learned a great deal from my errors. Regret came in large doses only when I wanted to act but did not out of fear of rejection or, even worse, failure.

Everywhere I went as a youngster I found adults following rules that had been passed down through the generations. Many of them had no basis at all in what was real. For example, I heard it said thousands of times that "It takes a long time to really know someone, and even longer to know if you love the person." But my own inner voices always told me quite the opposite. I could tell in a few moments that I loved a person and I knew that I didn't need the "test of time" to verify it for me.

Nevertheless, I was always being criticized for saying, "I love you" too soon. "You don't know me, how could you really know you love me? If it's that easy for you to say, how can I know I am really special?" (As if being special had anything to do with elapsed time, or, even more absurd, if one loved more than one person, somehow neither, instead of both, was special.) I abandoned the rules to which others paid so much tribute, and I became the subject of much consternation throughout my life. Nevertheless, despite attacks on my character because I chose to live by my instincts, I found that I was never disappointed in ME for trusting my first impulses when it came to

how and when I loved others. It was always others
who had the most difficulty with my quick assessments of whom I could or couldn't love. On a first
meeting, a first date, or a first anything, others were
always careful to say only the right thing while I
blithely went my way trusting myself and proud of my
ability to ignore rules about how one ought to feel.

It was this instinct for trust that was working for me
in the bleak hotel room on Uranus. I had only seen an
image of this woman called Eykis on the television
screen, and yet I knew that I loved her. She was someone I could trust to give me an insight into her people.
Although she seemed so familiar that she could have
been from my home town, she was my first contact on
Uranus with anything dramatically different from
what I had known on Earth. The anxiety attack report
that she delivered with such concern was the new element. This was my first moment of genuine inner excitement. Until then I was disappointed at this planet
called Uranus, modeled after Earth. Or vice versa.
Did we model ourselves after them? I ruled that out
right away. On Earth we certainly had no anxiety attack reports. I was going to find out, right from the
person who delivered that report, everything I'd need
to know to file my own account of the residents of
Uranus. I was thrilled at the thought of it, since until
then I had figured that my final statement on this entire
visit, this project of assessing Uranus in all its many
facets, would be summed up in a report composed of
one word: "Ditto."

I knew that "ditto" would not impress my fellow

Earthlings. If nothing else, Eykis was going to save me from having the distinction of being the first space traveler to file a one-word summation. I dozed off thanking this Eykis lady. My instincts were finely tuned. Tomorrow I must find and talk with this marvelous woman whom I knew instinctively that I loved.

2 · Eykis

She was the most approachable person I had ever encountered. I called the studio just once the next morning and we set up an appointment for four o'clock in the afternoon. Neither of us made any clumsy effort to be polite, and she didn't hem and haw about a busy schedule. I had planned an entire scenario to make myself as convincing as possible, but she made everything very easy.

"Hello, is this Eykis, the person who gave that anxiety attack report on the evening news yesterday?"

"Yes."

"I'm a visitor here, and I'd very much like to meet with you as soon as possible," I said, offering her every opportunity to refuse such a brazen request politely.

"What is it you would like to know?" she asked.

"It's very difficult for me to explain over the telephone. I would really appreciate it if we could meet.

You can be sure there's no danger," I said to reassure her.

"I'm sorry, what is that last word you used?" she asked.

"Danger," I repeated.

"I'm not familiar with that word. What does it mean?"

"I mean I wouldn't cause you any harm. I simply want to talk with you."

"Again you use a word with which I am unfamiliar. Harm? What is this harm and danger you use?"

"Would it be all right if I explained them to you when we meet in person?" I asked.

"Certainly," she responded, as if she were confused but still willing to discuss the matter.

"What time is convenient for you?" I asked.

"I'll meet you at four this afternoon. I'll come to your place, since you are visiting and perhaps unfamiliar with the transportation." There was not a trace of suspicion or doubt in her voice.

I gave her the name of the hotel and that was it. In three hours I would be holding my very first conversation with an inhabitant of this place called Uranus. It was becoming increasingly obvious to me that my initial assessment of Uranus as a replica of Earth was incorrect.

I jotted down three items in my notebook:

1. Anxiety Attack Report?
2. No concept of Danger?
3. No concept of Harm?

I thought about the phone conversation with Eykis again. She hadn't doubted me for a moment. There was absolute trust implicit in her voice, and she had made it all so easy.

I spent the rest of the afternoon walking about the city. Again I was searching for anything that would provide me with a clue to the uniqueness of Uranus. The differences that would have made my discovery more impressive were minimal and not really noticeable without careful scrutiny. I did not want to spend my time as a tourist, and the idea of uncovering subtle distinctions was obscured by the excitement of my forthcoming meeting with Eykis. She was the person I was counting on to give me honest answers to my questions and unlock the mysteries for me. I began to see the folly of looking for external differences. I had noted some, but I decided I would stop looking for outward appearances on which to base my investigation. I would follow my own instincts and listen to the people themselves. I would focus on Eykis. I simply could not get her innocent honesty out of my mind.

We spent three hours together that afternoon and evening. When Eykis left, my faith in the old bromide "Don't judge a book by its cover" had been renewed. Uranus might have all the external trappings of my home planet, but in fact it had almost no resemblance to Earth. Before meeting with Eykis, I had spent my time trying to unlock the secrets of a culture without looking into the one thing that constitutes a culture in the first place, the people themselves. I had stared blindly at the externals, instead of going to the source.

All the information we have about Earth's prehistoric people is based on the same mistaken principle. We leap to conclusions about these people on the basis of their artifacts—their pottery, hunting tools, homes, and so on. Would I want to be assessed and understood on the basis of the car I drive or the shape of my eating utensils? Does a fork tell anyone anything about me? I use the fork because I was taught to do so, but I could also use my fingers, or anything else available to get the food into my stomach. When the car isn't working I walk or hitchhike. But what does any of that tell you about *me?* Very little, of course, yet we make many absurd assumptions about Neanderthal Man without having any more information about them than our forks reveal about us.

I knew that our collective knowledge about all cultures prior to our own was infinitesimal, and yet I had begun my visit to Uranus with the same erroneous assumptions. I had studied Eastern philosophy extensively. I knew about looking inward, I had even said many times to acquaintances, "It's not what happens around us, or to us, but within us that really counts," but when it came to applying it, I had slipped miserably. After three hours with Eykis I would never forget that truth again. By seven o'clock at night on my second day on Uranus, I had stopped looking at the external similarities between our two worlds. They had become meaningless.

I shall never forget my first conversation with Eykis. I asked her if she would mind if I taped our talk. She had no objections. In fact, during the more than three hours we were together, she did not object to anything. I decided to begin with total honesty. I explained who I was, how I had arrived, and what I was doing on Uranus. I devoted several tense moments to trying to explain as clearly as possible, hoping that she would believe me and that she would not feel threatened, or want to turn me over to the authorities, who would subject me to endless questioning. (I simply couldn't get rid of my parochial habit of seeing the inhabitants of Uranus as I was, rather than as they were.) Eykis did not appear surprised at what I told her. Without flinching, she asked me what I wanted to know. I suppressed a strong desire to tell her all about Earth and, instead, asked what I thought would be a startling question.

"Why do you believe me? How do you know that I'm not lying and haven't come to exploit you in some way? I could be a kook of some sort."

She looked genuinely puzzled. "I don't know what you mean by lying," she replied. "Please explain."

Suddenly I was on the receiving end of my own clever salvo. "Lying, you know, not telling the truth," I responded.

"But the truth is all there is," she answered quickly. "How is it possible not to be truthful?"

"Well, if I were trying to hurt you, and as a way of deceiving you I said I was an Earthling here to learn about you, when I was actually intent on harming you, that would be lying," I responded.

"Well," she replied, "you now have the first difference that you can record for your report. On Uranus, people cannot do that. We are not equipped for, as you say, lying. Everything that everyone says is the way it is. Here on Uranus we can only operate from what is real. Why would anyone ever even want to lie? Wouldn't that make talking with each other impossible?" she asked, looking perplexed.

"But people on Earth don't always lie," I said. "Only sometimes when it is necessary or convenient."

"If people lie to each other sometimes, how do you know when they're lying and when they're telling the truth? Do they announce beforehand which is a lie and which is truth so that they can communicate with each other?" she asked quite seriously.

"It would break down the purpose of lying if one announced it beforehand," I said.

"Well then, I take it that people don't communicate truthfully on your planet. I wonder how that's possible," she said.

"Let's move to another area," I suggested.

"Are you lying or telling the truth?" she wanted to know in all seriousness.

"I'll give you my pledge," I answered. "I won't lie to you ever."

"Welcome to Uranus," she said. "But could you please tell me what you mean by a *pledge* and also by *ever*."

"Well, a pledge is a promise to tell the truth," I offered.

"So now I understand why we have no such word here. And *ever*?"

"When I said I won't lie to you *ever*, I meant from now on. As long as we know each other. Forever I will never lie."

She seemed even more bewildered. "This idea of *ever* and *forever* is new to me. All I know about is now, and it's enough for me to know that you will not lie to me now. I can't imagine how you can know what you will do, as you say, *forever*. But if that's how you feel now, it sounds fine to me. Please know, however, that if you change your mind before forever arrives, it is also fine with me."

"But forever never arrives," I protested. "It is forever."

"So if it never arrives, we're both talking about the same thing, the now. I guess we needn't discuss it any further," she concluded.

I was becoming exhausted because of my inability to phrase my thoughts and questions to accommodate her strangely sensible perceptual mentality. I was becoming bogged down in my own confusing questions and answers. She showed no exasperation, only mild befuddlement at my inconsistency. Her logic was inescapable, but surely they couldn't have built an entire planet so identical to Earth and still be so reality-based that she didn't understand simple concepts like lying, forever, pledge, danger, and harm. Of course, if they didn't exist for her, could she understand them? But wait, I was capable of understanding concepts that didn't exist for me. Perhaps Uranus people were inferior after all. I certainly knew about war, and I had never been in one. And I knew about God without unquestionable evidence. I made a note to ask about these things at a later time. For now, I wanted to get back to the business at hand, without becoming stalled in a maze of petty discussions about obvious language barriers. (Or were they my *limited thinking barriers?* I was beginning to consider this a genuine possibility.)

"Just what is an anxiety attack?" I asked her out of the blue.

"Anxiety sweeps over us quite regularly. It attacks in substantial amounts when the winds are right. We broadcast the likelihood of anxiety attacking, and in what amounts, as a public service," she stated matter-of-factly.

"But what is it?" I asked incredulously.

"Anxiety travels in the air in the shape of tiny microscopic particles shaped as little As, Ns, and Xs, hence it derives its name, anxiety. These anxiety particles were discovered by a scientist working with a powerful microscope. His name was Nopain, and therefore the most famous antidote for warding off anxiety attacks was named after the discoverer."

"But what happens if the anxiety attacks and you are without your antidote, as you put it?" I asked.

"Anxiety can take many different forms. If it attacks in large quantities and you are without your medicine it can actually break down your nerves into smaller pieces, causing what we call an N.B.D., or nervous breakdown. Generally, though, it attacks in milder proportions and the effects can vary from a general feeling of uneasiness, to nervousness, fear, paranoia, stammering, increased blood pressure, tension, and so on. Since the effects of an attack can be devastating, all newscasts announce impending anxiety attacks, so that people can take the proper precautions. Does this answer your question?" she asked with obvious concern.

"Yes, yes, it does, but it creates a thousand more." My mind was racing with thoughts. I'd never expected such an explanation. Anxiety actually attacked people on Uranus, and she couldn't be lying because she didn't even know how to do it. A strange, strange land indeed! "How often does it attack?" I asked.

"It's very difficult to predict. We can never make prognostications for more than a few days. It tends to almost sneak up on us. Therefore we have to be ready at all times. We can go for months without any attacks and then have three or four in one week," she responded.

I was beginning to see that this was a really singular phenomenon. I made a two-part decision on the spot. First, I would ask Eykis for another meeting as soon as possible, and if she were willing, I would then invite her to visit Earth, so she could see how anxiety was produced in another reality. But I would have to break that to her gently.

Before I could launch into the hundreds of questions swirling around in my mind, she turned the tables on me. "Don't they have anxiety attacks on Earth? You seem so flustered by my description."

"Yes, we do have anxiety attacks," I attempted to explain, "but anxiety doesn't attack exactly. In fact there is no such thing as anxiety per se. People just have anxiety attacks without anxiety actually attacking."

Now she was definitely puzzled. Yet she did not judge me, or appear to be agitated. "Well," she continued, "do they have antidotes for this mysterious anxiety that doesn't attack?"

"Yes," I replied, "we have tranquilizers, sedatives, therapy, and many drugs to cure our anxiety attacks."

"You keep saying that the anxiety doesn't attack yet you call them anxiety attacks."

"Correct," I countered, almost ashamed to say anything else.

"So how do you know when you are being attacked by anxiety, if by your own admission it doesn't attack?"

"We feel an anxiety attack coming on," I responded.

"From where? How? What are your clues?"

"We start feeling nervous, tense, and out of sorts," I offered.

"But these are the results of an anxiety attack, not the cause," she argued. "How can you feel tense when you don't have anxiety to attack you?"

"As I said, we feel it coming on."

"From where?" she asked in an exasperated tone.

"From within, I guess," I answered hastily. I was not at all certain of my logic by this time.

"But if it comes from within, it isn't an anxiety attack at all, but is simply anxious thinking. You wouldn't need medicine for this. Instead you'd need to change your thinking, wouldn't you?" she asked. "It seems so simple. What a blessing it would be never to have anxiety attacking us. Tension, fear, anxiety, and the like would all be gone if it didn't attack. Why do you choose anxiety on Earth if there is none to attack in the first place?" she asked, this time pausing long enough for me to answer.

I couldn't give her an intelligent reply. In fact, I had

the distinct feeling that I had yet to give her any answer that could be termed intelligent. "Can we pick up this conversation on anxiety attacks at another time? Can we talk tomorrow, or is tomorrow a concept that doesn't exist for you, since you are only here now?" I asked, not wanting to be sarcastic, but still feeling a bit shaken by her anxiety attack repartee.

"Of course tomorrow exists," she reminded me firmly. "But one cannot live or feel there. On Uranus, one can only live this moment. Even when we talk about tomorrow, we still only get NOW, but we can use up our NOW in any way we desire. Unless of course you're afflicted with *worry-wares*, or you can afford to purchase a *guilt-prodder*, which are the only two exceptions."

I almost laughed out loud at her worry-wares and guilt-prodders, but I could see that she was speaking in all seriousness.

"Before you tell me about worry-wares and guilt-prodders, would you agree to meet with me one more time?"

"I'll meet with you as many times as you like, but only if you'll tell me all about your place called Earth. It seems very strange, almost as if you can live each day in a reality that doesn't exist for me. I want to learn as much as I can about your odd homeland," she said.

I was about to protest, but I stopped myself and instead agreed to tell her all about my planet. I spent an hour telling her everything I could think of that really seemed significant about Earth. I told her about the seemingly duplicate proportions of our two planets regarding all external objects. She accepted this without the least reaction and never brought it up again. To her the fact that Uranus and Earth looked exactly alike on the surface was reality. Yet when I began to tell her about the people and our behavior, she appeared incredulous. She looked mystified when I told her about wars and prejudices; and when I talked of marriage, divorce, religion, and education, she looked at me as if I had three heads. As I rambled on about the pursuit of money as a way of getting ahead, she interrupted me.

"Do they have neurotics like we do here?" she inquired, almost as if she were following a line of questioning.

"Of course we have neurotics. We have a world full of them."

"And do they have the symptoms of neurosis, as we do here on Uranus?" she asked impatiently.

"I'm not completely sure about your symptoms, but neurosis tends to afflict almost everyone on Earth in a variety of ways."

"Such as?"

"Some people worry about their lives and they end up with ulcers, hypertension, headaches, cramps, and other ailments," I said.

"And they don't have worry-wares?"

"I've never heard of worry-wares, so I'm assuming that is something unique to Uranus."

"Well, if there are no worry-wares . . .' but she stopped herself, having already participated in this illogical discussion and having seen it go nowhere

"Tell me about your neurotics." She chose to learn rather than lecture or argue with me on this point.

I told her as much as I could about how Earthlings tend to live in either the past or the future. How they swallow tablets to cure depression and how most of them are dissatisfied with themselves. I went on about how people are interminably chasing success and are rarely satisfied, how they are troubled with the affliction of acquiring *more*. How so many suffer from unnatural fears called phobias and how few genuinely love themselves and even fewer are able to give love to others without qualification.

I told her of shrinks (a word she'd never heard except as a treatment for hemorrhoids) and how millions of people on Earth go to therapists for help. I talked on and on about anger, procrastination, free-floating anxiety, and self-contempt. She took it all in, and each time I talked about a different kind of neurotic behavior, she seemed to relax. But she was taking notes herself, and as seven o'clock approached, she asked me for another session.

"We have all of those things and more here on Uranus," she replied. "I think where we differ dramatically, if I am deciphering these past few hours correctly, is that on Uranus we seem to have a reason for all our neuroses. From what I can discern from this brief session, you also have neurotics on Earth, but I've yet to see that their neuroses have causes based in reality. I don't wish to jump to conclusions, so let's hash it all out tomorrow and then, if what I suspect is true, perhaps I could go with you back to Earth and see for myself. Since I'm exclusively reality-based, perhaps it will do me good to see how one can actually be neurotic without a reason based in reality. I'm puzzled by all this, but I'm willing to keep an open mind if you would like me to accompany you."

She had actually invited herself back, almost as if she knew that was what I'd been thinking. We said goodbye, and when she had departed I lay back on the bed unable to contain my delirium. I had much to think about in preparation for our meeting tomorrow. I dozed off with her words ringing loudly in my head. "Perhaps it will do me good to see how one can actually be neurotic without a reason based in reality." Now that was a thought I had never considered before.

3 · Second Visit

I had made my decision in the middle of the night, after spending hours dissecting our initial conversation and replaying her strangely logical statements. I had to encourage her to make the trip to Earth so she could experience the vast differences in thinking between our peoples. I would do everything possible to persuade her to visit Earth, but before doing so, I had to learn as much as I could about her and what to me was an alien way of thinking.

I had made peace with the external geography of Uranus. I accepted it as a virtual carbon copy of Earth. But all the talk yesterday about having a reason to be tense, neurotic or unhappy left unanswered questions. I just couldn't understand that her reality could be so different from mine. I had seen her people acting in a multitude of self-defeating ways and I was curious beyond description as to how she would explain what I had observed. I had done some reading overnight. I had also observed a wide spectrum of Earthlike human behavior in the people of Uranus. I had watched them in traffic jams, supermarkets, and family restaurants. I'd taken careful notes and placed an asterisk next to behaviors which paralleled those I had seen so often on Earth. I was aware of an entire catalogue of neurotic or self-deprecating behavior by her people, and I could hardly contain my self-praise as I contemplated questioning her about the flaws in some of her logic. She claimed to inhabit a totally reality-based world and yet I'd seen a great deal of remarkably Earthlike neurotic activity since I arrived.

The items that I would raise during the interview were well thought out, with many examples to indicate that the reality-based world described by Eykis had its own share of unreal, neurotic casualties, just as we did on Earth. We decided that this interview, in the course of which she would answer all my questions and collect my contrary observations about her people and her assertions, would take place over dinner in the hotel restaurant.

She appeared bright and full of smiles as we sat down at our table. "I'm sure you have many questions to ask after our marathon session yesterday," she said before I had an opportunity to say a word.

"I certainly do. I'd like to get started immediately, if you don't mind. I accept what you said yesterday about anxiety attacking and I can see why your people would use such a phrase as 'I'm having an anxiety attack,' if in fact anxiety does attack. Moreover, I recognize that anxiety does not attack on Earth, and people are still subjected to their own anxiety attacks.

If you'll accompany me back to Earth, perhaps you'll find the answer to that puzzling question. As for me, I've never had an anxiety attack, so it does not apply to my life. But would you please explain what you meant by worry-wares and guilt-prodders, before I do have my first anxiety attack?"

"But there is no possibility of an anxiety attack tonight, I've double-checked the forecast," she reminded me thoughtfully.

"All right, forget it, what about worry-wares?" I asked.

"Don't you have worriers on Earth?"

"Yes, almost everyone worries at one time or another, and we even have compulsive-neurotic worriers who do it all the time."

"And you don't have worry-wares on Earth?" she wondered aloud.

"I've never heard of a worry-ware in my life," I replied emphatically.

"So what is it that causes you to worry on Earth?" she asked.

"People just do it. They worry about getting sick, about airplanes crashing, about their families. It's a way of life."

"But what causes people to worry?" she asked, growing more impatient at what she must have thought was evasiveness on my part.

"Well, people cause themselves to worry, I suppose."

"And what do they get out of worrying? Does it keep them from getting sick? Or their loved ones from having an accident? Does it prevent planes from falling out of the sky?'' she wanted to know.

"No," I replied. "Worry doesn't stop anything from changing. People have just learned to do it.

"Why would they use up their precious moments for living by worrying about something they can't do anything about? It seems so pointless." She was clearly perplexed.

"So what are these worry-wares you've mentioned? Are they some kind of invisible bacteria, like anxiety, that force people on Uranus to worry?" I asked.

"Oh, no," she replied, almost startled at the absurdity of my conclusion. "Worry-wares are a technological advance on Uranus. If something is going to happen in the near future, such as an airplane trip, or a sickness, worry-wares can give you an exact forecast of what will happen if you follow a particular course."

"You mean they can actually change the future, these worry-wares?"

"Not at all." There was a tone of exasperation in her voice. "They work like this. Let's assume that I will spend a few minutes worrying about my plane trip next week. I will write down the worrisome thoughts and program them into the worry-ware computer terminal. The computer will tell me how the flight will turn out. If I'm told that it will crash, I can alter my plans and avoid that particular flight."

"But why doesn't everyone simply use the worry-ware computer terminal? If they did they would never have anything to worry about."

"Of course almost everyone does use the information in the worry-ware computer, but it still doesn't eliminate the need to worry."

"How so? Please explain," I implored her to continue with this odd explanation.

"I've just told you. You must first worry in order to get the information you need. Thus on Uranus we all have an absolute need to worry in order to avoid having catastrophes befall us. Doesn't it work like that on Earth?"

"Not exactly," I replied, knowing that this was the highest level of understatement one could ever achieve on any planet.

"You did say that almost everyone on Earth worries, didn't you?"

"Yes, that's correct, but on Earth worrying can never aid anyone in looking into the future. That is quite impossible in our reality system," I said.

"Then why do you worry?" she asked again, with that all too familiar tone of befuddlement in her voice.

"Perhaps we had better wait for your visit to Earth," I stalled again in my cleverly evasive way, so as to avoid appearing outright stupid by stating the real answer that was turning over and over in my mind: I just don't know. "So worry actually serves a great purpose on Uranus," I offered in my superfluous way of summing up.

"Tell me about those guilt-prodders you mentioned earlier," I suggested. I was hoping that I might find something there that I could use with my own family, since they were almost all veritable guilt machines themselves, either dispensing it on the one hand or unabashedly embracing it on the other. As usual,

Eykis first asked me if we had such a thing as guilt on Earth.

"In enormous amounts," I replied. I assured her that few people on Earth had escaped the clutches of guilt and that it ran the full gamut, from feeling horrible about having disappointed members of one's family to feeling awful about getting a free ride by failing to push when going through a revolving door.

"Well, guilt on Uranus is very common also, and without it I can't imagine how we would survive. It is a most useful and sought-after commodity indeed," she answered, leaving me sitting there with my mouth wide open, trying to predict what she would say next about the virtues of guilt on Uranus.

"How can guilt be useful?" I asked, wondering what she would throw at me this time.

"Without guilt, we would never be able to go into rewind, and hence we'd be forever stuck with our behavior as it occurred the very first time."

"Rewind!" I exploded. "How can you accomplish rewind?" I almost shouted, drawing the attention of other diners to our table.

"You can't tell me you don't know about rewind. I've seen you use it repeatedly with your tape recorder. Whenever you want to go backward and replay something, you go into rewind," she argued.

"Yes, but that's on a tape recorder. People can't do that!"

"Not exactly as you do, since your rewind button restricts you to replaying whatever transpired exactly as it was done originally. A guilt-prodder is not a limited one-dimensional machine like your tape recorder.

It enables you to go into rewind when you feel bad about something, and you can correct your error."

"Do you mean that people on Uranus can rewind their life experiences and correct them at will?"

"Not without guilt they can't," she replied.

"So that feeling guilty can actually put you into this position called rewind and then you do something over?" I asked, hardly believing what was coming out of my mouth.

"Of course," she answered almost laughing at my incredulity. "If you couldn't do it over, what good would it do to feel guilty about it in the first place?"

"Hold it right there," I insisted. "Where does one get one of those guilt-prodders?"

"You don't have to 'get one,' as you put it. All Urantians are given one on their third birthday. I just don't see how we could survive without them."

"How do they work exactly?" I demanded, becoming impatient with her cool, almost superior tone.

"If you do something that you dislike, such as use abusive language to your parents, you close your eyes and just feel guilty for forty-five seconds, then—"

"Hold it," I interrupted. "You just feel guilty, what does that mean precisely?"

"You know, you think guilty thoughts. That's all guilt really is, thoughts that give rise to particular feelings and behaviors."

"What kind of thoughts, for example," I asked.

"Thoughts such as . . . I wish I hadn't said that . . . I feel terrible about having been short-tempered . . . I'm really a bad person, and so on. You know, guilty thoughts," she said.

"Then what happens?" I wanted to know.

"Your guilt-prodder activates your rewind button and you can go back to the initial encounter with your parents."

"And you mean to tell me you get to re-do the abusive conversation?" I had almost shouted again. I would have to control the volume of my voice or risk having the meeting ended by a maître d'.

"Certainly, only this time you speak as you feel you should have the first time, and then it's all behind you."

"And what purpose does the guilt fulfill?" I asked, wanting to make sure that I was hearing correctly.

"That's quite evident," she said, "without guilt you can't activate the guilt-prodder, and without the guilt-prodder you can't go into rewind. Consequently, we all need guilt in order to correct our behaviors."

"But what if you do something really terrible, like steal, or even hurt someone?" I asked.

"Same principle applies," said Eykis. "You use your guilt-prodder, go into rewind, and re-do it. Then you learn from your behavior and program yourself not to do it again. But people do not hurt each other on Uranus in the sense of causing them what you call harm. You see, with the small exception of rewind, our reality dictates that we live only in the present moment. When people are living fully in this moment, there is no need to cause hurt or pain to others. There are times when we say or do things that we'd like to correct, hence we have guilt and rewind. But actual harm is not possible, since there is absolutely nothing to gain from it. We have only this moment, no more, no less.''

"That's incredible. On Uranus you actually need guilt in order to learn from your past," I said.

"Of course," she offered. "And don't you have rewind for people, just like you do for your tape recorders?"

"No," I said solemnly.

"But you do have guilt," she asked with emphasis.

"Yes, we do," I said even more solemnly.

"And guilt is painful, just like it is here on Uranus?" she asked, apparently wanting to be certain that we were talking about same commodity.

"Very much so," I replied. "People on Earth are often obsessed with guilt over what they've done."

"But if they can't go backward and correct the behavior, what's the use of feeling guilty?" she wondered.

"Well, the guilt helps to remind them how bad they feel, which in turn teaches them to avoid repeating that behavior," I offered feebly.

"But," she countered quickly, "if the guilt is painful and it doesn't help you re-do what you did, why don't you simply learn from your mistakes, bypass the guilt, vow to avoid that behavior in the future, and have no guilt as a bonus?" she asked.

"I—I don't know," was all I could think of to say.

"Doesn't your guilt simply immobilize you?" she asked.

"Yes."

"And no amount of it can ever get you to go into rewind to correct what you've done?"

"Yes again."

"Then it seems to me that it's one thing to do something you dislike and feel bad about it, and it's quite another to do something you dislike and carry guilt around with you. It's double jeopardy, for crying out loud, and it also seems irresponsible to me," she said.

I had never thought of guilt as irresponsible before. I asked her, "How is it irresponsible?"

"Obviously, if you are just going to choose an emotional reaction which is going to be painful, and at the same time isn't going to lead to a correction of the behavior you detest, then guilt immobilizes you and keeps you feeling terrible to boot. To me that's irresponsible."

"But isn't your guilt also irresponsible?" I asked. "Don't you feel bad when you do things you dislike, and isn't that called guilt?"

"Guilt on Uranus is necessary in order to correct what you have already done, therefore it is a most responsible choice. On Earth, from what I can gather from your questions to me, you can't replay your past, so I would think it essential to learn from your mistakes, correct them in future encounters, and sensibly shun the painful guilt. But then, I have difficulty imagining a world without guilt. As painful as it is for a few moments, it still serves such a wonderful purpose. No one on Uranus would be without his guilt-prodder, I can assure you."

I was impressed. I must say, greatly impressed. Just as with her worry-wares, she was able to make an eloquent defense of guilt because it was functional. I was beginning to see what she meant by being in a reality-based culture. If an emotion didn't serve a purpose, she simply didn't use it. All the guilt that I had heard defended throughout my life seemed utterly pointless in the face of her logic.

I asked Eykis about conversations I had overheard on Uranus in which people said the same foolish things I had heard so many times back home. I gave her a list of sentences which included:

"You should have done it this way."
"You wouldn't be having this problem if you'd only listened to me."
"You shouldn't have done it this way without consulting me."

When I confronted her with the absurdity of such postulations, she acted surprised at my having pointed them out.

"Should-have, would-have, and could-have are very valuable tools," she explained. "They influence someone to activate the guilt-prodder and ultimately get into rewind."

"In what way?" I asked.

"By saying 'you should have,' obviously people are telling other people that they didn't do something as well as they might have. The recipients may then choose to feel guilty and re-do it, so as to please themselves and behave more effectively in rewind."

"But what if a person feels that he or she did it just the right way and doesn't like that should-have," I asked.

"Why, the recipient simply ignores the 'you should

have.' You see, the purpose of 'you should have' is to give the option of re-doing. If one were unable to go into rewind, there would be no sense in telling another person 'you should have.' "

"But, Eykis," I protested, "what if you really disliked what someone did and you felt that person would have benefited by doing it your way? How would you possibly inform anybody of the need to improve?"

"You mean, assuming the person can't go into rewind and re-do it?" she asked.

"Yes, yes." I had forgotten about that damned rewind thing here on Uranus.

"The answer is so simple that it hardly bears saying. You would tell the person to work at not repeating that foolish behavior in the future. You would never say 'you should have,' since it serves no purpose. But a life without rewind is difficult for me to imagine."

"How do you handle criminals if you have no use for guilt?" I asked.

"I didn't say we had no use for guilt, *you* are the one who apparently has no use for it. On Uranus, guilt is quite useful and criminals do not exist. Anyone who behaves in a way that is contrary to the law is required to accept responsibility for his behavior. Guilt helps. It makes one rethink what he or she has done, then go into rewind and correct the wrong behavior. Anyone who refuses must take responsibility for it."

"Just how would a person do that?" I asked.

"Quite simply," Eykis said. "Someone who has stolen property must return it and pay restitution. Those who refuse are incarcerated and permitted to work on construction projects that benefit everyone.

such as roads, libraries, schools, and all sorts of public service. Those who refuse to do such work live in solitary confinement until they choose to be responsible. But our prisons are virtually empty, since going into rewind through guilt eliminates the need for incarceration. It is a rare occasion when a person chooses not to go into rewind in order to act in a law-abiding manner the second time, or to be responsible through work projects. Since these are such sensible choices, solitary confinement is almost never used."

"But what about violent crime, in which someone elects to harm or even murder another?" I asked.

"These concepts of harm and murder don't exist here, since we are strictly reality-based. No one on Uranus is capable of even wanting to hurt anyone because it serves absolutely no purpose, unless there is a rare dependency-diode malfunction which I'll soon explain. We know intuitively that each person has a right to be what he chooses for himself. Consequently no one can choose to alter anyone else's humanity. I assume by harm and murder you mean altering someone. We can't do that, it simply isn't within our reality to think and behave in the ways you've described as harmful."

"But don't you think a person who could do that, and there are many on Earth who can and do, should be made to feel guilty?" I asked.

"Not if the guilt cannot activate rewind," she said almost instantly.

"But shouldn't they be made to repent and correct their ways?"

"Now you sound like you live here on Uranus. Repentance is internal and voluntary, behavior is external. Changing a person's ways in the future is possible. But why should that have anything to do with guilt? Can't a person learn, repent, and grow, or even be confined, without the accompanying guilt?" she asked.

"I'm not sure," I replied.

"Well, I can tell you for certain that if guilt didn't lead to rewind, it would never exist here on Uranus. Even if we had violent crimes against each other, guilt wouldn't help to rehabilitate anyone and would very likely encourage repetition of the offensive behavior. As I said earlier, either you go into rewind and correct the behavior while learning from it or you suffer society's punishment. However, the guilt won't correct anything when you don't have the rewind option."

"If everyone is reality-oriented and can go into rewind to erase mistakes, why did I see signs of the same social problems on Uranus that we have on Earth? What about your prisons and abortion clinics?" I asked.

"Those particular terms may apply on Earth. What you saw were houses of correction and women's centers. On Earth perhaps these titles are merely euphemisms for the coarser terms. On Uranus they are quite literal. People occasionally commit acts which cannot be accepted by society; they would correspond to 'harming' someone on Earth. Because of malfunctions in dependency diodes or other explainable dysfunctions, a person may refuse to go into rewind. He will need counseling to see why his actions were in error. A house of correction is a rewind counseling service in a live-in establishment. It *is* a *house*. It is for *correcting* errors in thinking. In reality, the people are not bad, they're just wrong.

"Women's centers deal with all phases of a woman's life. There are programs for physical fitness, sex education, general medical problems as well as gynecological needs, fertility, pregnancy, nursing, and child care. There is something of interest to any female of any age for body, mind, and spirit. With rewind, we don't need abortions, but there are classes and counselors to help women think things through so they don't have to make rewind decisions on a regular basis. And, I might happily add, there is no social stigma against anyone who chooses to bear a child, regardless of the circumstances. The child will not suffer, either."

'Explain why the news report I saw when I first arrived carried stories about drug centers. Why would such places exist in your culture?"

"Again those are literal, descriptive titles. All chemicals not acquired from food are available only through a drug center. The doctors and pharmacologists keep track of medicines prescribed for illness, and of vitamins and other aids for people on holistic programs for maximum levels of vitality and health.'

This made some sense to me, and I didn't want to get bogged down in having her "defend" her reality But I still had one nagging question about that evening news report.

"What viable reason could there be for all that military equipment? I saw film clips of military academies where young men and women in uniforms were training, and why did I see aircraft carriers and submarines along with swarms of troops using what looked like artillery, if you have no concept of harm in your world?" I was proud of my keen observations, and I almost hoped I had found a discrepancy in her otherwise flawless logical explanations of the behavior of her people.

"My, my. Appearances are deceiving, aren't they? Your descriptions are most vivid—and, I'm delighted to say, truly inaccurate. Through science we've controlled the instincts for territory, aggressive protection of the species, and the need for combat as a proof of strength and power to select the dominant leaders. That may have been important originally for survival of the fittest, but in rational moments we know that it not how we want our society run today. To give the 'inner animal' a chance to express itself without causg injury to others, we have war games, which are run like our Urantian Olympics. The military academies you thought you saw are not for training fighters out athletes The aircraft carriers do carry aircraft. It saves fuel in getting the equipment to the competitions. And some of those planes are only good for short-range flights; they'd never make it across the ocean.

Submarines participate in undersea competitions, but the skilled crews are really training for future employment at oceanic fish farms where subs herd the schools of tuna the way cowboys herd cattle. Other marine crops growing on the sea floor are cultivated and harvested by submarine. The Games are very good and practical training grounds.

"As for the artillery troops, you may have seen shooting, but it was at targets, not people. They take turns covering the same territory so the points can be given fairly. The big artillery, pointing skyward, shoot fireworks displays. They are judged on originality, variety of color and form, theme, combined effects of sound and light, and so on. The finals are always at night. You must have seen a film clip on practice drills. The timing is so complicated. It's really very technical, intricate, skillful . . . Why are you laughing?"

"I'm just imagining what would happen at the next summit if we proposed doing away with all nuclear arms and substituted a fireworks display."

Her thinking was always so impeccably sensible. Worry and guilt existed on Uranus because they were useful. Inhabitants of Uranus did not harm each other because it served no purpose. Anxiety attacked and therefore the need for tranquilizers. We moved away from all this talk of guilt and I asked her about something I had noted everywhere on Uranus—people talking about their phobias.

"Of course we have phobias. They're a terrible problem, but we've learned to tolerate them. It's part of our reality, if you know what I mean," she said, referring to her reality in a cute manner with the slightest hint of a smirk.

"I overheard someone on the bus say these exact words to her friend," I said. I reminded Eykis that I had recorded the conversation on tape so as to be exact. "The lady said, 'Elevators really frighten me. I'm afraid to ride in them anymore.' Now I ask you, how can anyone who is reality-based, as you put it, say something so unreal? Obviously elevators don't scare people."

"Have you ever ridden in an elevator on Uranus that was programmed to scare you?" There was not even a trace of a grin on her face as she spoke, so I knew for certain that she wasn't joking.

"Programmed to scare you—why? For what purpose?" I asked.

"Here on Uranus elevators are built with speakers ir them. When the programming shifts to 'scare,' and it can do so without warning, the speaker emits a frightening sound, sort of a creaking, high-pitched wail. It can really give you the shivers."

"So why not just eliminate the eerie noises and rid yourself of this phobia?" I wanted to know.

"Because scary elevators are the antidote to that stupefying taped music. Elevators are built that way and most people learn to adjust to them and it isn't really that bad. But for some, elevators really are terribly frightening." She looked puzzled again. "Don't people have phobias like fear of elevators back on Earth?" she asked quizzically.

'Why yes, of course, but the elevators themselves don't scare people. It's the attitude people have toward small, closed spaces," I offered, knowing what was about to be asked and knowing also that I wouldn't have a sensible answer, again.

"So that's why you were so surprised to hear our people say 'elevators scare me.' You never heard it stated like that, right?"

"Wrong, my friend Eykis," I replied. "I hear it all the time."

"But you just said that elevators on Earth are not programmed to scare anyone, and if that's the case, why would anyone on Earth ever blame the elevator for a fear of enclosed spaces?" she asked, almost dumbfounded at the direction the conversation had taken.

I decided to ask about other phobias, since I had nothing to say that would clear it up other than the same old safety clause that I had used too many times by now. "You'll see when we get to Earth."

"Let's forget about elevators for a moment. Do people on Uranus suffer from acrophobia?" I asked.

"Certainly," she replied. "Heights really scare people here, it is a very serious and common phobia."

"Just how can a height frighten anyone?" I asked.

"Heights simply do not want people exploring them. It is our way of life and everyone knows it on Uranus."

"But how can a height want anything? It's nothing more than a high place," I insisted.

"Not on Uranus," she snapped, "and you wouldn't be saying that if you had ever gone too close to the top of a mountain or the edge of a cliff."

"Are they equipped with scare programming like your elevators?" I asked. I was beginning to feel stupid for even asking such questions.

"No, there is no programming for scare, but the tops of our mountains and all our cliffs are on hinges," she said.

"What!" I shouted from total disbelief.

"Now don't tell me that you don't have hinges back on Earth," she said.

"Of course we have hinges, but mountains and cliffs certainly are not hinged in any way."

"Well, if they aren't hinged, how can they come off?" she wanted to know.

"Why in the world would a mountain top want to 'come off'?" I asked, almost losing my patience with the silly direction in which the conversation was headed.

"Didn't you tell me earlier that you had heard someone, several people in fact, saying heights scare them?"

"Well, yes." I admitted that I had heard it many times, and had even recorded it in my log of things to ask about.

"So how would it ever be possible for anyone to say such a thing if the cliffs and mountain tops weren't on hinges? When people get too close to the top or the edge, their weight may activate the antiavalanche control system and cause the peaks to swing out on hinges with a sudden whoosh. That's how heights scare you. How else could it be done?" she asked.

"Has this ever happened to you?" I asked her.

"No, sir," she said emphatically. "Heights have never frightened me, how about you?" she asked of me.

"Well, we don't have any hinges on our mountain tops and cliffs, that's for sure," I answered.

"Well then, we're alike in this matter at least. I guess you've never heard anyone say 'heights scare me' before," she said.

"Ahhh, yes, as a matter of fact, I've heard it many times, but let's save it for another day. I'm sure you'd be even more confused if we really dug into the matter."

All these wonderfully strange conversations had me smiling inside as I contemplated what it was going to be like for Eykis back home on Earth. All she understood was so insanely sensible. All she knew was her own reality, and I was beginning to see how it was indeed, in so many ways, light years removed from the reality I had learned about on Earth.

Back home I was considered a highly evolved, no-limit kind of person. But here on Uranus I'm sure Eykis was beginning to think I was a genuine Loony Tunes character. I decided to plunge ahead with our interview, to learn all I could that night. She had told me that this would be her last opportunity to speak in depth, since her work was piling up. She had also said she was putting everything in order so that she could accompany me back to Earth for a brief two-week observation of her own. All my talk about anxiety attacks without anxiety attacking, elevator phobias though elevators were not programmed to scare people, and other mysterious happenings had piqued her interest in my place of origin. She was clearly interested in seeing it firsthand.

"Will your family object to your leaving without taking them along?" I asked.

"I won't allow them to be upset," she said innocently.

"But how can you allow or not allow someone else to be upset?"

"I'll hide their feeling-hurters and disconnect the anger terminals from their portable units," she said, as I almost literally picked myself up from the restaurant floor.

"Okay, okay, I give up, what is a feeling-hurter?" I asked in amused wonderment.

"You mean to tell me that on Earth people can't hurt other people's feelings?"

"Of course they can, it happens all the time, but what has that to do with a feeling-hurter?" I asked.

"Once again you puzzle me, but I'll restrain myself until I see your people with my own eyes. I can't imagine how anyone can hurt another's feelings without the benefit of a feeling-hurter. But to answer your question, a feeling-hurter is a very light-weight portable machine which you carry on your belt or in your purse. It comes in many different models depending on how much you're willing to spend. The typical feeling-hurter has three buttons specifically programed for basic family members. One is for siblings, one for parents, and one for grandparents or anyone else who may be living in the home. You can order more expensive varieties that include in-laws, co-workers, and even strangers if you want to spend the extra money."

"But how do they work?" I wanted to know.

"They operate through invisible lasers. If you want to hurt your sister's feelings, for example, you aim it directly at her, and zap! You push the button marked sibling and she'll generally respond in a whiny tone, 'Mom, he just hurt my feelings.' Make sense?"

"Sense," I exclaimed. "It's absolutely phenomenal. You mean that on Uranus one cannot hurt someone else's feelings without a feeling-hurter?" I asked.

"How would it be possible?" she shot right back. "How could anyone hurt someone's feelings without a feeling-hurter?"

I didn't want to go into it. So I simply shrugged off her rhetorical questions and put it into that ever growing category of "Wait and you'll see when you get to my house."

But I must say I did think about her question long and hard. I knew that Eykis, who was already greatly baffled by my inability to answer her questions intelligently, would not be satisfied with my reply. Maybe a visit back to Earth would clarify things for her, although I was already beginning to be certain that her visit would only confirm her recent conclusions about us Earthlings.

"So your family won't be able to have hurt feelings about your trip because you are going to hide their feeling-hurters," I restated, to be sure I'd recorded it properly.

"Either I'll hide them or I'll disconnect the wife/ mother terminals. They would be inconvenienced to be completely without their feeling-hurters for two weeks, so I'll just disconnect those lasers that would affect me."

"Amazing, absolutely amazing," was all I could say. "And those anger buttons you mentioned, do they work in a similar way?"

"Almost exactly," she replied, "except that they aren't portable. Anger is too serious an emotional response for people to be carrying around anger-provokers, so the terminals are fixed within the home. The government restricts the sale of anger-provokers because they can be dangerous. Although no one would, as you say, 'harm' anyone else, still, a provoked attack of anger can create things like tantrums, shouting, kicking inanimate objects, and the like. So we seldom use our anger-provokers. But you can definitely make someone else angry here on Uranus by pushing the right combinations of buttons.''

"So you are going to insure that your family isn't upset at you by actually tampering with their buttons, so to speak.''

"I will simply inform them that I don't want them to hurt my feelings. I don't want them to make me angry and vice versa. Then I'll show them what I've done and no one will be hurt. Can you suggest a way to handle it any better?'' she asked quite sternly.

"Not at all,'' I replied without hesitation. "You really have a terrific plan there. In fact, I'd love to take some of those toys back home with me.''

"You mean that you don't have feeling-hurters and anger-provokers on Earth?'' she wanted to know.

"Right again, Eykis,'' I said.

"So no one can make anyone angry or hurt anyone else's feelings on Earth. Right?'' she asked, almost hopefully.

"Wrong again, Eykis,'' I said.

"I know, I know. We'll wait until we get there,'' she said. I feared that she was anticipating some kind of alien technology that would help explain Earthling thinking and behavior. She was in for a shock.

It occurred to me that without their mechanical instruments, the people of Uranus would never suffer the pain of anger or insult. Why introduce such destructive emotions into society? I wondered. I asked Eykis directly.

"Much earlier in our history, we found that without a range of emotion we had no stimulation for creativity. We were exceedingly dull. This technology was as wonderful an advance as, say, the automobile. But, like cars, it got out of hand. With cars there is the tendency to get a bigger, faster, newer, more complex model every year. That was becoming the case with feeling-hurters and anger-provokers. Competition and status dictated the purchase more than actual need. Now there is government regulation, as with auto emissions and so on. Our scientists seek alternative devices also, just as we investigate mass transit, but the use of these emotion zappers is deeply rooted in the society and won't change until a clearly superior system has been proved to be effective and readily available."

"Aren't your family members somewhat dependent on you? Won't they miss you while you're gone?" I asked, changing the subject from feeling-hurters and anger-provokers.

"Dependency is very important for young children. How else would they survive?" she asked me right back.

"I'm not talking about very young children. I'm talking about young people who can think for themselves, who would survive without their parents, teenagers for example. I'm also talking about adults who become dependent upon each other within the family. How about that?'' I asked.

"I see. Well, in almost all cases we disconnect the dependency diodes from our young children about the age of eleven, and then dependency—absolutely relying on anyone else—is impossible. I must admit, however, that some people on Uranus do have dependency needs beyond age eleven, often well into adulthood, and occasionally throughout their entire lives.''

I now felt as if I had finally gotten hold of something I could relate to. This was very Earthlike, and I didn't want to let it go. "So why would anyone want to remain dependent after he is able to think, feel, and live as an independent-thinking person?'' I asked, almost as if I were a prosecuting attorney who had finally trapped a key witness and caught him in his own illogic.

"Haven't you ever heard of defective dependency diodes?'' she asked, showing her disdain for my prosecutor-like tone. "Dependency is like an illness. We don't get angry at people for being sick. No one can help it if he has defective dependency diodes. The person to whom it happens usually remains dependent for a while. Rather than thinking for himself, he often wants others to do his thinking for him. He blames his parents for his problems and in fact he is right. Only parents control dependency diodes and a miscalculating parent can create a dependency that might even last. Fortunately, all the dependency diodes are operating properly in my family. I have a whole group of people in my family who can think for themselves, who never blame me for their problems, and who share and love each other very much. I'm thankful that all my dependency diodes disconnected properly. With the exception of my husband's jealousy-jam, which he rarely uses, we have a wonderful family of interdependent and independent functioning people. No one wants to put the control of his life in anyone else's power, since that would take away what we prize most on Uranus—freedom. But we must thank the skillful parents for disconnecting the diodes flawlessly. Believe me, I've seen families where everyone is dependent and obsessed with loyalty to the unit, instead of loyalty to being individuals within the unit. This can be a nightmare. But it's all in the hands of the diode manipulators.'' She stopped and looked at me. I knew what was coming. Sure enough . . .

"You look bewildered again," she said. "Tell me, how could there ever be any dependency, as you put it, when the diodes are working properly? Don't tell me . . ."

"You guessed it," I murmured.

"You mean no dependency diodes on Earth?"

"You said it."

"And you still have dependencies in people after age eleven?"

"Yes indeed, but before you swallow that one, let me ask you another question," I begged her.

"Okay, shoot," she said. She was picking up my Earthly vernacular.

"I just let that jealousy-jam thing go by. What do you think I'm thinking about that one?"

"I'll bet you've never heard of jealousy-jam, and

that you still have jealousy on Earth. And that I won't be able to comprehend how that is possible until I see it for myself when we get to Earth next week. How did I do?'' she inquired.

"You've got it one hundred percent correct," I said, "and I am even going to try and tell you about this jealousy-jam I've never heard about," I stated, taking pleasure in our role reversal. "When your husband wants to make you jealous, he puts this jam on his toast and eats it, then he is jealous, right?"

"Almost," she said, stifling her laughter to avoid being impolite. "First, you don't eat jealousy-jam. You simply rub some on your fingers. And second, you don't make yourself jealous with jealousy-jam, you make someone else jealous. So my husband would rub some of the jealousy-jam on my fingers, or vice versa, and then he would be able to say, 'You're making me jealous.' You see, the cause of neurotic behavior is always located in the other person. Jealousy-jam on my fingers makes him jealous. Jealousy-jam on his fingers makes me jealous. Got it?"

"Why would he *want* to be jealous?"

Eykis dropped her gaze for the first time and blushed rosily. "It is the finest stimulus for arousal," she said with honesty and embarrassment, struggling for control of her constricted voice. "We enjoy convincing each other there is no cause for jealousy in reality."

I grinned. "That's one jam I'd like to try, then!" I teased.

She smiled and relaxed. "I'm sure you would," she

said, able to resume her usual unwavering eye contact. I felt myself reddening this time.

"You know," I said, "what really scares me is that I think we are beginning to understand each other."

She smiled and wanted to know if I knew enough yet for us to begin the preparations for our visit to Earth.

I was thrilled that after so many hours of being together we had finally figured out, although only in a minute way, something about our separate, unique realities.

"Before we close," I almost pleaded, "let me ask you a few more questions. I think I know how your reality is indeed separate from ours, but I want to verify it for myself."

"All right," she answered willingly. "And I'll suspend my questions for you until we get to Earth. But to be perfectly honest with you, I must admit that while I am exceedingly pleased that you're seeing how my reality system works, I am more than confused about how yours works. I just can't seem to understand it. Everything seems so alien. You tell me repeatedly that you have the same emotional reactions we do, and yet I've failed to grasp how or why you get them. But I'll be patient. There must be some sensible explanation that simply eludes me at the moment."

She was definitely wrong about the sensible explanation. But I didn't want to say or do anything that might discourage her, or add to her bewilderment. We spent another hour talking about almost all the topics on the list of things I wanted to know. I'd learned by now to suspend my disbelief and I was no longer surprised at what appeared to be absolutely ridiculous assertions. I'd finally given up trying to see her through my own reality. I accepted her for what she presented herself to me as being. I'd finally learned to stop judging her and to see that she was incapable of distorting the truth. Eykis was in fact the personification of an accepting human being, living comfortably with the reality of her society and eager to grow with each new experience.

I had read a great deal about no-limit people firmly entrenched in their own reality. They seemed to be superior human beings who could transcend themselves and all their petty concerns and involve themselves in a strong sense of purpose and mission. They were reality-based people who never forgot the vital truth of what is. But Eykis' truths were so new to me; so foreign. I'd forgotten that a person's reality is just that, and that it is not something to scoff at but something to enter and accept. Still, even I had to admit that this was a very different reality. Gadgets and jams, lotions and diodes, anxiety attack reports, and more. But so what! Isn't the reality of a supposed schizophrenic just as unbelievably bizarre and unreal? And hadn't I learned long ago that walking in someone else's shoes was far more reality-based than pretending that their shoes were unwearable?

Eykis allowed me to view myself objectively. She made it possible for me to see my prejudices and judgments by demonstrating that she was incapable of the same prejudices and judgments. She showed me her world, and I'd wasted my energy in being flabbergasted and incredulous. In the time that Eykis and I had spent together I learned as much about myself as about Uranus. Mostly I'd discovered that my disbelief in her reality was related to a simple fact. *I was attempting to understand her as I was, rather than as she was.* I vowed to stop this kind of assessment. I had prided myself in never behaving that way with anyone on Earth, and yet I was being as ethnocentric as I could be with Eykis on Uranus. Consequently, when she said things that would have shocked me only yesterday, I reacted with calm resolve today. I was beginning to understand her reality and that understanding came from listening, not arguing or even questioning.

As she told me about blame points, calculated by blame bankers, I understood what she was saying. Blame points were assigned by blame banks which informed the government division. Taxes were paid accordingly. On Uranus it made sense to blame. Self-rejection lotion was also easy for me to consider now. Some people actually used it to stimulate self-awareness. The end result was improved self-understanding, since self-contempt sloughed off with dead skin. I didn't question this sensible reasoning for so much self-rejection on Uranus. The lotion was available to cause these temporary problems, leading to positive results. Otherwise, as Eykis had said to me, "How else could you explain people participating in so much self-rejection?" She elaborated on the importance of fearing failure on Uranus. Fear worked in conjunction with those worry-wares and actually helped one to avoid failure by fearing it. Again, who was I to argue?

The second simple fact that accounted for my disbelief in Eykis' reality stemmed from its utterly sensible nature. Something was missing on this planet of Uranus even though it looked the same as Earth. I felt that the "missing link," so to speak, was precisely what gave my own planet its distinctive (and unfortunate) character and history. Everything seemed to have such a common-sense explanation. On Uranus, people had reasons to be neurotic. The reasons were tied to their reality. In contrast, I could never think of a reason rooted in reality for anyone on Earth to be neurotic or even unhappy. And Eykis' incredulity at my inability to give a sensible answer was quite disturbing to me. She couldn't grasp an "unreal" or senseless explanation, her reality simply didn't provide for it. Yet, she was always polite and willing to wait and see. It was when she talked about love and loving, sex and sexuality that she really touched my soul. Such a simple definition, so easy a concept. I knew as I listened over and over to what she told me of love and loving that I'd never even experienced such a joy, nor had I known anyone who ever had. Not on Earth at least. And most frightening of all, I didn't know if it was even possible to experience it in my reality, unless Eykis showed me the way. But that, too, was impossible to consider. I wouldn't want to even chance my dependency diode being defective, or having her use jealousy-jam on me . . . or would I?

• Part Two •

EARTH

4 · First Observations

As Eykis and I had agreed before we left Uranus, she was to have ten days to travel over our entire planet when she arrived here on Earth. She would travel inconspicuously and alone. There would be no hoopla concerning her arrival, in fact it was to be kept a secret, just as my visit to Uranus had been. She wanted to see with her own eyes, without my assistance. She was emphatic in her insistence that she have the freedom to observe and interact unobtrusively, to research and ask questions, all on her own. She assured me that she was capable of seeing everything in ten days, since that was all the time available to her. She had agreed to record her observations on tape and note any questions she might want to ask me.

As soon as she arrived, Eykis used the *Urantian Formulas* to pull the greatest disappearing act I had ever witnessed. We had agreed on the time and place we would meet within ten days and I knew she would keep her word. She didn't know how to do otherwise. Keeping her word was a part of her unique reality.

My first inclination was to worry about her. I smiled inwardly at her description of worry-wares and wished I had access to the little device she had described on Uranus. I would have loved to peek ahead and be certain that she would be safe, but I recalled what she had said about worry. "Why would they use up their precious moments for living, by worrying about something they can't do anything about? It seems so pointless." I suspended all worry thoughts and decided to use the next ten days productively.

I sorted out and tried to organize the tapes and voluminous notes I had made. She had talked to me about so many things. I felt overwhelmed trying to write it all down in a single coherent volume. I had thought about the importance of her messages. How wonderful it would be if I could somehow introduce this phenomenal way of thinking and feeling to the people here on my planet. I envisioned a world in which people used their minds to wash away the foolish and unnecessarily destructive thoughts that ruin so many lives. I visualized importing some of those funny gadgets Eykis had described and shown to me. But we had enough negatives without them.

I was back on my comparison excursion again. It was so difficult for me to simply see Uranus as it was. I still wanted to argue with it, to prove that its inhabitants were wrong and we were right. Not once had I ever heard Eykis imply that we were inferior. To be sure she found us confusing, but she had never insisted that we be otherwise. I did so much want to take advantage of this new knowledge, to apply it in some way to help my people escape their collective obsessions with taking drugs for their problems, or seeking answers in therapy or some silly encounter group or in gurus of every description. Somehow I knew that Eykis had secrets for me and all my people, but I wasn't sure how to tap them, how to have her share them with all of us. She had a singular kind of good sense that, if used properly, could literally transform our world.

I thought about her constantly, wondering how she would fare traveling about this huge planet. I knew she wouldn't be an alien to our physical world, since she had lived on our twin planet all her life. But the surprises that were in store for her, even though I had spent days briefing her, were surely going to be monumental.

"They're wrong!" she shouted as she burst into my room at the hotel at our agreed-upon time.

Hadn't I just said to myself that she never even tried to prove us wrong? This was a shocker. She bounced around the room, almost ranting.

"What? Who's wrong?" I blurted, without even saying hello.

"I've discovered the reason behind the rampant unhappiness here on Earth," she said, still waving her arms and walking around the room. "I've talked inconspicuously to many people, but mostly I've simply observed. I've listened to people all over your world, in Asia, Europe, Africa, North and South America, and even the islands in the Caribbean and South Pacific," she said, and paused to catch her breath before continuing. "We both know the concept of neurosis. We have it on Uranus, and you have it here in the same proportions. You have as much unhappiness here, and your people rarely talk or act as if they are fulfilled. It all stems from one basic flaw. The problem is not that you are unhappy, or even unfulfilled, the problem is that you are almost all wrong." She had calmed down, but her excitement at this alarming discovery did not decrease her enthusiasm for what she was saying.

"If you want to teach your people to be happy and fulfilled, you must teach them to be correct!" she said.

"What do you mean by correct?" I asked, not wanting her to lose track of this thought.

"Look," she said, "you saw anxiety, jealousy, phobias, fears, and self-rejection all over Uranus. You observed people aiming their feeling-hurters and causing others to be embarrassed through their embarrassment barrels. You saw it all. That is simply our reality. We accept our reality and then set out to be happy and fulfilled within that reality. If our reality can be altered, we work at altering and feel purposeful in the process. But on Earth, everywhere I went I saw people thinking, feeling, and behaving in ways that were simply inconsistent with this reality. Almost all the people I saw thought and acted as if they were privy to a reality different from that which exists. Yet they always ended up being done in by the only reality there is. They were wrong, wrong, wrong, and for the life of me I can't figure out why they simply didn't start thinking, feeling, and behaving right, right, right!

So you tell me, Mr. Earthborn, why all this wrongness?''

I had never seen Eykis like this. Her confusion had finally won out over her sensibleness. She was hammering her fist on the table, demanding both insight and answers. She wasn't angry, or even upset. She had used this word "wrong" several times and I wanted to know more about what she meant by it. I'd known she was in for some shocks, but I hadn't expected this "They're wrong!" reaction to be so overwhelming.

"Let's go back a bit," I implored. "What have you seen that has led you to conclude that we're wrong?"

"In my first few days I discovered that there are many small but important physical differences between our two worlds. However, this was of little concern to me. I noted that your military equipment fired real bullets and that your jails contained people who were put there because of the 'harm' they might cause themselves or others. I noted the locks on your doors and the guns in your homes. These, and all the other strange paraphernalia of a violent world, were not surprises to me, since I am well aware of our own ancient history on Uranus.

"I viewed these physical differences as problems of evolution. Eventually, through experience, you will find that it is quite possible to eliminate these destructive elements in your world. You will be able to use your prisons and submarines for positive purposes when you have finally experienced the futility of competing with each other and have moved to a more advanced form of living together, called cooperation.

This will come when you're ready for it, and just plain unable to tolerate the violence. My biggest shock comes from the wrongness of your thinking.

"I'll start with my first observation, which occurred in a bank line last Monday morning. I was simply going to get some cash, as you had suggested, when I overheard two women in front of me having this conversation. I taped it for my research as you encouraged me to do. Here's an exact transcript."

FIRST WOMAN: "My sister never should have moved to Florida twenty years ago. If she'd listened to me, and not married that oaf, she wouldn't be having these problems today."

SECOND WOMAN: "Well, she should have listened to you. But you know how younger sisters are, they have to prove themselves."

FIRST WOMAN: "She shouldn't have left her family like that. If she'd done what she was supposed to, she wouldn't be going through a divorce now, and she probably wouldn't be stuck with all those children and I know she wouldn't be seeing a shrink either."

SECOND WOMAN: "How is she feeling now that she's talking to a psychiatrist?"

FIRST WOMAN: "She's still miserable because she just wouldn't listen to me twenty years ago."

SECOND WOMAN: "Well, she has a right to be miserable, having gone through what she has."

FIRST WOMAN: "You're right, she does have a right to be miserable. But she wouldn't be that way if she'd taken my advice when she was twenty.''

"There you have it,'' said Eykis, ''I didn't think too much about it at first, but after a few days of observing your planet, I could see that this entire conversation was plainly and simply—WRONG! I'll bet I've listened to it fifty times, and all I can conclude is that these two women, for whom this was a perfectly normal, healthy conversation, were incorrect about the very nature of their own reality.''

"In what way?'' I asked Eykis.

"In the first place, you were right about rewind. It is strictly limited to tape recorders. People here don't have the ability to re-do their errors.''

I didn't say, "I told you so,'' but that's what I was thinking. However, I was feeling some empathy for her frustration at trying to make sense out of her very first conversational eavesdropping on Earth.

"Well, all of this 'she should have,' 'she shouldn't have,' is simply wrong. Tell me, without rewind and guilt-prodders, what purpose is served by rehashing what you should or shouldn't have done?'' she asked rhetorically.

She paused a moment and then continued talking without waiting for my response. "And besides, it's *over*. If you can't re-do it on this planet, as I'm beginning to see, it *can't* be redone. That being the case, why would anyone ever say, 'she should have,' 'shouldn't have,' 'wouldn't have,' or anything even resembling it?''

"Eykis, please, it's just a figure of speech. It

doesn't really mean what it sounds like," I said unconvincingly.

"But it's a figure of speech that derives from incorrect thinking, it makes people unhappy. I mean those two women . . . the first one especially, became more and more enraged as she talked about the should-haves. The little homilies that people here use in speaking are rooted in fantasy. Can't you see that?"

"Look, I'm not defending it. I agree that it sounds pretty ridiculous when looked at through your eyes," I said.

"But I'm not looking at it through my eyes, I'm seeing it through their eyes, and they're wrong about their reality. If I saw it through my eyes, I'd be teaching them how to fix the sister and go back twenty years. But you can't do that here," she said.

"Well, what troubles you so much about their being wrong?" I asked, because she did appear to be genuinely concerned.

"What troubles me is that when people are wrong about their reality, they're trapped in their own self-imposed shackles. As long as they continue to be wrong, they can never escape. It's not that this particular conversation made the two ladies unhappy. It's that happiness is always impossible when you see your reality incorrectly."

"Go on," I said, sensing that she had more to say on the matter.

"Don't you see, my friend—" She almost grabbed me. "They didn't say, 'She made those decisions and now she'll have to live with the consequences and perhaps change if her decisions aren't working any longer.' What the woman said was, 'She should have listened to me,' and 'She shouldn't have moved away.' Unless I am as wrong as most Earthlings, it seems to me that on Earth you simply cannot 'shouldn't have' done something that you've already done.''

"You're correct about that," I assured her.

"But still, I heard this conversation over and over. On a Friday afternoon I heard a clerk from the phone company tell a customer who wanted his phone fixed that day, 'You should have called on Wednesday,' and the man accepted it. He walked away as if she had said something that made sense, that is, something correct. But they were both wrong and equally unhappy with their lives at that moment. I wanted so much to whisper in his ear, 'On Earth, you cannot 'should-have' called on Wednesday, on Friday. It just cannot be done.' But I recalled our agreement and acted only as an innocent bystander. For now!''

I wondered immediately what she meant by "For now!" But I let it pass.

"You are right, Eykis," I said, "you cannot 'should-have' called on Wednesday, on Friday, but you can call next Wednesday, and that is very likely what the clerk was trying to convey. In a snooty kind of way, of course," I offered as a partial explanation.

"But you don't understand. She wasn't interested in helping him get his phone fixed. She was intent on giving him a lecture and keeping the problem as a problem, rather than seeking a solution. And the worst part is, he bought it! He walked away shaking his head and saying, 'I didn't know I should have called on

Wednesday; I guess it is my fault.' Here were two people communicating with each other, and neither was tuned into Earth reality. How can a whole planet do this all the time and not fall apart?'' she asked.

But before I could answer her, she glanced back at the transcript on the table. ''And furthermore, why would people ever say anything like 'She has a right to be miserable,' almost as if they were arguing *for* the person's unhappiness and defending her limitations at the same time?''

I had no response. Eykis was upset about what she had seen. As she explained later, she was hurting for all these Earthlings who were so unnecessarily unhappy. With her own unique kind of reality-only orientation, she couldn't grasp why people thought, felt, and behaved as they did. She even confided that if she could just get everyone to stop being wrong (nothing else—just stop being wrong), there would be no neurotics on this planet, since from what she could ascertain there were no real-world reasons for being that way. She was the most idealistic realist I had ever faced.

She asked me for a simple explanation of the two items she had observed in the initial conversation she had overheard. (1) the *should-haves,* without benefit of rewind leading to re-do, and (2) the *"right to be miserable."* Rather than try to explain away these seemingly harmless conversational habits, I acknowledged that they did indeed represent wrong assessments of our reality. But I still failed to see why she was making such a big deal about it. After all, these weren't desperately unhappy people she had observed. They were typical, everyday, normal folks in everyday Earthly conversation. As I relayed this thought to Eykis in the hotel room, she looked at me with more than a trace of sadness in her eyes.

"That's the very point I'm making, my new-found friend. Don't you see how widespread being incorrect is in your world? If it's so blatantly obvious in an innocuous discussion between two women in line at the bank, or a customer asking to have his telephone fixed, it means that the entire planet is awash with this kind of thinking. It's the everyday common folks that I wanted to observe. It is they who provide the clues for understanding a people. If they are infected with this 'wrong way' disease, then it is very likely that it is even more widespread in the influential echelons of your world. If the business, political, and educational leaders suffer from being wrong, and if they implement their false thinking in carrying out their duties, then it can literally trickle down to all segments of your world. And it obviously has, since little old ladies in bank lines are so blatantly afflicted."

"But don't you think you're jumping to enormous conclusions based on a couple of insignificant chit-chatty talks?" I asked hopefully.

"It is precisely the little chit-chatty talks, as you put it, that are the most revealing," she said without blinking. "But don't forget, I've been observing most intently all over your planet and I've merely reported my very first encounters. I have a whole suitcase here filled with tapes and written observations. My conclusion about neurotics simply being wrong comes from an entire inventory of Earthly behaviors. Before I offer you what I think will be a remarkable set of gifts to all of the people on Earth, I would like you to see the rest of my notes, perhaps go through these tapes and maybe even supply answers that are still missing.''

I agreed. Obviously I was thrilled to be a part of witnessing the results of her apparently thorough ten-day exploration of our planet. I loved the way she looked most of all when she was perplexed and rambunctiously excited at the same time. She was a fireball of high energy and she conveyed it in everything she said, even in her little personality quirks. Her eyes always flickered before she presented me with one of her discoveries. I loved the way she jumped up in her enthusiasm or pounded the table with her fist for punctuation. I also loved her simple honesty. The way she always spoke in no-nonsense straight talk. Eykis never pulled punches. One always knew what she wanted to convey.

I sat there, with her, deep in thought about how absolutely lovely, no, perfect, she was, and yet I didn't even notice her outward appearance. The things that one usually refers to in saying that a woman is ''lovely'' weren't even on my mind. I only wanted to focus on just WHO this remarkable woman was inside, not how she looked. I was excited by something that she had said earlier and I had almost glossed over. ''A remarkable set of gifts to all of the people on Earth.'' I thought she herself was the essence of just that, but I knew she had something else in mind. I was also aware that she would share it with me when she, rather than I, was ready.

She came out of her deep thought and asked that we put off further talk until the next day. She had spent a week traveling and recording her observations. She was exhausted and yet I knew she would never complain to me. Back on Uranus one didn't complain to others about fatigue, one rested instead. There simply was no complaining in her reality.

As she stood up to leave, after scheduling a full day with me the next day, she told me that her visit to Earth was more than half complete. She wanted one more meeting with me, and then we would make arrangements for her final days here. She asked that I think about how she might best be utilized. As she held the door slightly ajar, I kissed her ever so lightly on the mouth. Nothing sensual, simply our very first touch. "I think I love you, Eykis," I said somewhat clumsily.

Long ago I had learned to say that familiar phrase if I felt it intuitively. At this moment my intuition was working overtime. She reacted with the most unique response I've ever heard.

"I know you do, and you can be sure I am aware of *what that means now,* as well. I'll see you at nine o'clock tomorrow morning. We have much to learn from each other. Good night, as they say here, as if a night could really be *good* or a day *bad*."

5 · Eykis' Final Observations

There was no doubt that we were becoming closer, despite her efforts to approach her task objectively, almost scientifically. Eykis still showed unmistakable signs of emotion, signs in which I wanted to read a deeper meaning than was intended. But then perhaps it was only thinking on my part. The brief time that I had known her had been the most stimulating in my entire life. No exceptions. I had spent weeks in the company of supposed gurus from India and Tibet. I had studied ancient Zen masters and talked directly to modern ones. There simply was no basis for comparison. Eykis was a breed unto herself. Her communication was so alarmingly simple that it almost knocked me out before I could digest it. The only comparison that even came close was some very special moments I had spent with young, unspoiled children. I have a reverence for children. I have always felt most at home with those young people who laugh, tease, and lay their emotions right out on the table for you to accept, reject, or handle as you choose. Simple honesty is always present in children, and Eykis had all the qualities characteristic of children as well as a profound knowledge of how to think realistically and the ability to articulate that knowledge with no nonsense. I always seemed to be thinking about her inner qualities. This was new to me. That was exactly what I was thinking as she bounced into the room early in the morning ready for our final day of sharing each other's observations.

"Let's walk this morning," she said in the straightforward style that was unique to her.

"All right, Eykis," I said. "Whatever pleases you."

We left immediately and walked through the city to the waterfront. As we walked together, stopping now and then at an occasional picnic table, we became consumed by our shared experience. It was becoming easier for me to touch her now, and once in a while I would take her hand in mine and just hold it while we walked. She never once offered any resistance, nor did she seem at all affected by my touch. She accepted it as my way of walking with her, and did not make an issue of it. Yet I relished being even closer to her. Somehow I felt that touching her brought us closer, and yet I knew it didn't mean that to Evkis at all. For the first time in my life that didn't bother me one iota.

"So what do you find most confusing about Earthlings?" I asked her.

"Well, I told you about my observation that most of you are simply sizing up your reality incorrectly. That is the one characteristic that seems present in virtually everything I've noted about your people,'' she said.

"In what other ways do you find that we are mostly wrong in assessments of our reality?" I asked, encouraging her to pursue this line.

"Okay, I'll get even more specific than I was yesterday. As you know, I give the anxiety attack report on television back home, and I think of my job as a public service, that is, important work which helps people to avoid anxiety."

"I agree with that," I said instantly.

"Well, on the logs I've kept since I arrived here on Earth, I've noted that well over a thousand times, in my limited sample, I heard people announcing that they were 'having an anxiety attack.' I've learned that anxiety does not attack on Earth, and furthermore, there is not even anything resembling anxiety on your planet. It just doesn't exist! Yet people are acting as if it did." She paused to catch her breath, then she continued. "I can only conclude that all the people who say or believe they're having an anxiety attack are just incorrect. Yet I don't know why they would choose to be wrong. You all have a choice in virtually everything you experience on Earth. So why, I keep asking myself, do these people keep choosing to be wrong? Then, by checking with your medical associations and experts in the health professions, I learned that tranquilizers and other drugs designed to quell anxiety are consumed in record numbers. But why is this so when there is no such thing as anxiety here on your planet?"

"Eykis, hold it. How can you say there is no such thing as anxiety on Earth. Just look at the people;

they're full of anxiety about their relationships, their job performances, the uncertainty of war, money, the economy, their health and on and on. We have plenty of anxiety.''

"Okay," said Eykis, "where is this anxiety that you speak of?"

"Why, just because you can't see it doesn't mean it doesn't exist," I offered meekly. "It's in the people themselves."

"Precisely my point," she countered, "anxiety per se doesn't exist as it does on Uranus. Here on Earth there are only individuals thinking anxiously, and that is quite a different kind of reality altogether."

"In what way?" I asked, not wanting to lose sight of this observation of hers.

"Why, in every way possible. On Earth, you control your thinking, and it is up to each person to decide for himself how he wants to think. This is your *corner of freedom,* so to speak. But instead of using that freedom to think in self-enhancing ways, you make two huge errors. First you elect to think anxiously, and then you blame the results on anxiety itself, rather than on your own choices. Consequently your people say things like 'I'm having an anxiety attack.' It is simply incorrect to speak this way, to say nothing of the thought processes behind such verbalizations."

"But is that so harmful?" I asked in all seriousness.

"It is devastating!" she said emphatically. "When people assign responsibility for their anxiety to some mythical anxiety attack, they need a second myth to correct the original. The second myth is that swallowing an antidote, such as a tranquilizer, will rid them of their imagined anxiety.''

"Okay, Eykis," I protested, "but what if people don't say they are having an anxiety attack, but simply feel anxiety because of the way they're treated, or because they encounter frustration as they try to reach their goals.''

"It is even more absurdly wrong and preposterous for a person on Earth to make such a claim. On Earth, regardless of how things are going, or, as you put it, how you're being treated, you still have absolute power over what you decide to think. This is your reality. Therefore, when all appears lost, or you're disappointed in others, you can still elect to think in either nonanxious or anxious ways. If you elect anxious, you end up tense, hurt, afraid, angry, or just plain hyper, which is not conducive to happiness or personal fulfillment. If, on the other hand, you elect to be nonanxious, you get an opportunity to correct or ignore the externals and have your fulfillment as well. Now if neither choice will change your reality or how others choose to react to you, why wouldn't all people here simply make the better and incidentally the correct choice?''

"When you put it like that, I don't have a reply, except to say that most people have learned to make the 'incorrect choice,' as you put it, because it's easier to blame someone else for their anxiety than to accept responsibility for it and rid themselves of it," I offered.

"That is precisely my concern," she said. "I have concluded that people on Earth want to avoid taking responsibility for their problems, including their anxiety. This gives them an excuse when it comes to doing what is necessary to change. As long as they continue to believe that anxiety comes from without rather than from within, they can never do anything to bring about happiness for themselves, and since they also go around drugged, their chances are minimized even further.''

"So you feel that this self-deception or 'wrong-way reality' can be the cause of total unhappiness," I asked.

"Yes, emphatically," she answered. "Not only does it preclude total no-limit happiness, but it can lead to even more devastatingly incorrect choices.''

"But how can anything be more devastating than an absence of happiness and no chance of reversing it?" I wondered to her aloud.

"I actually heard several people talking about their anxiety attack having led to a nervous breakdown," she told me.

"Yes, that can happen," I offered.

"But it can't happen on Earth, it is plainly an illusion," she answered.

"You wouldn't say it was an illusion if you'd ever seen these broken souls that reside in mental institutions," I reminded her.

"But I did see them, I visited them and talked with their friends and relatives," she replied.

"So you see, it's not an illusion, is it?"

"The results are not illusions, they are very real indeed. But that doesn't change the fact that the reasoning that got the people in the institutions in the first place is an illusion. First of all, nerves don't break down as they do on Uranus. I checked all the autopsy reports of persons who had actually died from these choices. I couldn't find one single report in which nerves broke down. The nerves do their job on Earth, and you don't know how lucky you are, compared to a real nervous breakdown à la Uranus. Second, the people who have these fictitious nervous breakdowns, which seem to be the final result of too many nonexistent anxiety attacks, don't really believe they chose their infirmities. They literally believe that someone else created this monster—and what is even more puzzling, the 'someone elses' also believe they are responsible for the anxious thinking of their friends and families. They feel guilty almost all of the time, without benefit of a guilt-prodder, which I've yet to see on Earth. These people actually are prone to illusional anxiety attacks of their own, which can even lead to their own mythical nervous breakdowns. It is indeed a vicious circle that stems from one thing: *incorrect thinking*. It is just plain incorrect for you on Earth to say 'anxiety attacks,' 'they make me nervous,' or 'I'm having a nervous breakdown.' Now how, please tell me,'' she asked, ''can I state it any clearer than that?''

"You can't," I admitted. For the first time I experienced the frustration that she must have felt with these incorrect Earthlings who could have it all as far as happiness and fulfillment were concerned. She knew that our reality, unlike her own, gave us the freedom to be whatever we wanted. I could almost hear her thinking, ''If we didn't have anxiety attacks, feeling-hurters, and the like, as integral parts of our reality, there would be no barriers to our potential happiness. Earthlings are a collection of people with no reason in their reality to be unhappy, and yet almost all of them choose unhappiness and blame someone or something else for their troubles." But she didn't say it. Instead, almost as if she knew I was reading her thoughts, she changed her tactics completely.

"Speaking of blame," she said, "there seems to be a lot of that here, and I've yet to hear of blame points or blame bankers."

I was reminded of our conversation on Uranus, in which Eykis explained the blame points, which were controlled by elected blame officials. Each person on Uranus was assigned a set number of blame points which were kept in a blame account at the blame bank. Thus when someone blamed another for his problems, or ascribed responsibility for his lot in life to externals, it was because he was reacting to his own reality the only way he could. That is, realistically. On Uranus people indulged in blaming because they had an allotment of blame points, and that was that. When I asked Eykis why they would have such a neurotic system, she had replied in a way that I didn't understand at the time, but that was crystal clear now.

"Do you question why you need fresh water for drinking, when 75 percent of the Earth's surface is salt water? Wouldn't it make much more sense to use salt water to drink? Why isn't your planet that way?" she had asked rhetorically, answering her own question instantly.

"You need fresh water because of your physical evolution, it is your reality. We have blame points, feeling-hurters, and everything else you find so incomprehensible because of our social evolution."

"You are right, Eykis," I said, shaking myself out of my temporary mental excursion back to Uranus. "Blame is definitely a common practice in our world."

"But again," she retorted, "it's an illusion. Blaming is always a reality error, and yet it's so commonplace here," she reminded me.

I tried to explain. "Don't you see, Eykis, blame is really quite functional. It enables people to blame others and avoid having to take risks. It makes it easy for them to explain why they are unfulfilled, and it reduces the options they have to change. It's really quite functional, even though it is certainly neurotic." I was feeling somewhat satisfied with myself. That was a pretty good explanation.

"Of course it's functional," Eykis responded, "but so would drinking salt water be functional, there's such an abundant supply. So why don't the people do that?" she asked.

"Well, it would kill them," I said. "People can't swallow salt water without being poisoned."

"I rest my case," she answered. "Blame and the resultant anxiety are just as poisonous to the psyche as salt water is to the body. People don't drink salt water because their reality won't permit it. When that same reality screams at them not to blame, they ignore it and imbibe the poison, blaming the poison rather than themselves for the ill effects. It's like blaming the mirror for what it reflects."

"Just what kind of blaming have you observed?" I asked her. She inhaled deeply, as if she were going to say a great deal in that one breath.

"Why, it's an international pastime," she exclaimed. "I heard a man respond to the question 'Why are you so down today?' with 'The stock market's performance depressed me. How can I be up when my stocks are down?' Now I ask you in all sincerity, how can a stock market control a person's emotions? I checked into the stock market and I found that it has no connection with human emotional conditions, yet I heard many, many people blaming the 'market' for their unhappiness."

I stifled a laugh at the absurdity of the image in my head: a stock market actually dispensing depression. She continued.

"I heard one doctor ask an obese lady, 'Who is responsible for your being so overweight?' She responded without even smirking (I thought she might be a public satirist): 'Sara Lee.' Then she gave another name, 'Big Bones,' I think, who had also made her fat. I checked out Sara and discovered that it's merely a bakery. Imagine, she believes a lady baker actually made her fat. I still have an asterisk next to 'Big Bones,' and I've been meaning to find out who that is, because from what I can discern, he or she is wreaking havoc on people's lives by making them fat."

I couldn't contain myself any longer. I burst into laughter at the image of someone called *Big Bones* rampaging the countryside and indiscriminately dispensing fat to the unwary.

"So what's funny about that?" she wanted to know.

"Again, Eykis, it's an expression that fat people use. And your suspicions are correct, there is no one called Big Bones here on Earth. People, in fact, elect their obesity through self-defeating choices, and then blame others for their conditions."

"This is so prevalent, I can hardly believe you don't see the folly of this way of thinking," she said.

"Anything else in this blame category?" I asked.

"Everything seems to be in this blame category," she replied. "It all seems to boil down to self-responsibility versus blaming others. Obviously those who accept responsibility for themselves and their lives are few and far between," she concluded.

"I'm sure you found some reality-based thinkers?" I suggested hopefully.

"Hardly at all, and those I did observe tended to be mostly blamers and only occasionally wandered straight into their own reality—realistically, if you know what I mean?"

"I do, but can you give me an example of those part-timers?" I asked.

"Certainly," she said at once. "I saw a man who appeared to be a reality-based person. He didn't blame others, he was happy and fulfilled, both physically and mentally. But when he was being loud and boisterous in a restaurant and obviously losing his temper because of the slow service, he explained his quick temper with one of the strangest comments I've heard here on Earth."

"Yes, and what was that?" I asked, not knowing what to expect.

"When his friends said, 'Hey, calm down, relax,

enjoy yourself,' he responded in all seriousness, 'So what do you expect from me? I'm Italian! I've always been that way!' Now you tell me what his being Italian has to do with choosing to be impatient! I checked what being Italian meant in reality, and it has nothing to do with his explanation. It means, 'from Italy, a country in southern Europe.' Nothing more, nothing less. But he uses it as his blame source.''

I smiled. ''You're correct, Eykis. People often blame their cultural heritage for their personality quirks. I guess it's just easier than taking responsibility for them. I'd never really thought of it before,'' I confessed to her, ''but people here do have a large say about their own personalities.''

''On Uranus,'' she said, ''people aren't given a choice in such matters. They are assigned the kind of personality they will have. But here it's entirely up to each individual to choose what he would like to be. At least that's what I have observed. Yet people act as if they had no choice at all in the matter.'' She was talking faster again, which she did when she wanted to hammer home a point.

''I've heard people blame their parents, their birth order, their ethnic background, their childhood, and on and on. Yet according to my investigations, it seems that even as very young children all Earthlings have, and always did have, the ability to use their corner of freedom, that is, to choose their thoughts.''

''But surely, Eykis, you don't think that Earth children choose their personalities? Don't you think parents do in fact shape and mold their children and, in

fact, are somewhat responsible for what they become?"

"My observations are admittedly limited. I've been
studying your planet full-time for less than ten days.
Nevertheless, I don't see the validity of the beliefs
expressed in your question," she said.

"How so?" I asked, listening most intently.

"I've observed large and small families, where, for
example, an alcoholic father is abusive to all his children. Some take it seriously and are afraid, others
ignore it, and others blame him for their shyness. To
me, if he were in fact creating their personalities they
would all be what he wanted them to be. Yet each one
is unique. Each reacts separately to his behavior.
Even as children they choose how they think. But
that's not the tragedy. The problem surfaces when
they grow up and look back to their childhoods for
explanations (that is, blame) of their adult lack of fulfillment, or unhappiness. Instead of saying, 'As a child
I chose to react this way or that way, and perhaps I
didn't know any better then, however I do know better
now, and if I don't like something about myself today
I can't blame daddy, because if I did then I would be
saying that I can't get better unless he changes.' On
Earth, what daddy did is over as far as I can tell, so
blaming him is, again, simply incorrect. He didn't do
it to you even then—you chose your childhood reactions. And if you continue to believe he did, you will
only remain unhappy."

"But," I offered, "wouldn't an understanding of
what he did help you to change more readily?"

"Why, of course, but it's not an understanding of

what he did that you're after. It's an understanding of what YOU did that really counts. Saying 'My father's alcoholism made me what I am today' is not an understanding. It's an excuse, and an incorrect one at that.''

"Then what would a correct understanding be?" I asked.

"Very simple," she stated. " 'My childhood reactions to my father helped to create what I am today. It's not his fault, he was only doing what he knew how to do. How can you ask any more of anyone than that? If shyness is my problem and I don't like what I've made of myself, I'm going to change being shy by practicing new nonshy behaviors.' Now on Uranus, with the benefit of rewind, guilt-prodders, and re-do, we could fix that up fast.''

She'd done it again. She had cut through the wishy-washy blameful thinking. Her sensible, razorlike logic kept her from employing excuses. Here on a planet where free will and personal choice are the only reality, she simply couldn't find any rationale for blame, particularly since she resided on a planet where free will was not taken for granted, and blame was dispensed by external sources. No matter how long we talked, she remained at a loss to explain why anyone would ever blame, when the results were always so destructive to the one doing the blaming.

We talked for many hours that day. I felt a new sense of awareness about my own potential for fulfillment and happiness. She was not critical of us, but thrilled and amazed at the abundance of our opportunities. She was such fun to be with. I would laugh with her at the folly of our ways, as she pointed to the significant differences between her reality and my own. I laughed hard when she told me about having overheard a conversation related to complexes.

"I heard a woman telling her 'shrink' that her husband had given her a complex and that consequently she felt inferior. She was blaming her husband for her feelings of inferiority, but I was getting used to this by now."

"What was it that you found so objectionable, if you expected her to blame her husband anyway?" I asked.

"At that time I wasn't aware that you can't enter a complex encounter study," she explained.

"What do you mean, complex encounter study?" I asked, surprised again by Eykis' seemingly impossible conclusion.

"On Uranus, if you want to deepen your relationship by working through a complex, you go to the Department of Encounter at the university and register for a complex encounter study. They issue one per spouse and you can earn credit toward a psychology degree while learning more about each other," she explained.

"Have you ever received a complex?" I asked Eykis.

"Why, certainly, my husband gave me one, for my breasts, many years ago."

"And how did it work? What did you do with the complex?" I asked impatiently.

"Well, I kept it for three years. Imagine, for three years I had a complex about my breasts. But that's the maximum time under the law for retaining a complex given by your husband," Eykis responded.

"But what was the complex? What did you do with it?" I asked.

"Well, I wore special underwear for three years. That reminded me to go around telling others about my inadequate feelings regarding my breasts. I looked in the mirror and felt inferior, all the things you do when your husband gives you a complex for your breasts." She was brutally serious.

"You must have been happy when the three years were up and you were finally rid of that complex," I said sympathetically.

"Well, I was pleased to earn the credits and I did acquire some insights into my husband's attitudes. Complex encounter study is simply a part of our educational system in the psychosexual department. When you enter a study project you accept it as basic to the learning technique. Besides, I gave him a three-year complex for a little portion of his anatomy, so it all worked out, as complexes usually do."

"Then you must have been in shock when you heard that woman telling her shrink about her husband giving her a complex, when they can't literally be purchased here as they are on Uranus," I asked.

"Of course I was shocked. I went to all the department stores asking for the 'complex department,' and they all thought there was something wrong with me."

The image of Eykis asking information-booth clerks for the 'complex department' was hilarious. We both laughed out loud at the absurdity of shopping for a complex. And yet the woman in her therapist's office really believed her husband had given her that inferiority complex.

These lighter moments were a treasure for me. They served to drive home Eykis' message that it wasn't the big problems but the little ways that we had learned to think, feel, and ultimately behave that made life miserable for most people on Earth. She made me see clearly that none of the big problems on Earth would exist were it not for the erroneous thinking that seemed to infect almost all of us. And she hinted that part of her package of gifts to me would be the opportunity for all of us on Earth to change these big problems. But I wouldn't press her yet. We laughed even more at her descriptions of the multitude of people with phobias, who blamed the things they feared for the fears themselves. She recalled an uproarious afternoon searching elevators for speakers programed to scare. She had not found any mountains with hinges; nevertheless she had still heard people saying over and over, "Heights scare me." She ended her frustrating attempt to find the causes of those phobias with the conclusion that people on Earth scare themselves and blame everything else so they don't have to change their incorrect thinking, which is really the cause of their fears. This conclusion came only after her frantic search for what she thought had to be the real causes of these phobias, in the light of her own reality-only approach to life.

"Would you like to hear another of my discoveries?" she asked, breaking a long silence during which we had both been lost in thought.

"I've come to the conclusion that most of the people on Earth participate every single day in self-rejection exercises, and I know you have no self-rejection lotion here, since I've researched the subject exhaustively." She seemed almost proud, like a little girl who had just received her first straight-A report card.

"That's quite a conclusion," I countered, wanting her to continue telling me about her remarkable discovery.

"And furthermore, I know now exactly why they do it, although I was really baffled by this behavior at first."

"Please fill me in on this discovery," I said. "Don't hold back."

"Well, it goes like this. Remember to correct me if you find any flaws."

I agreed. I must admit I was anxious to hear what she had concluded.

"People are trained, almost from birth, to dislike who they are. Young children are somehow expected to gain a sense of self-esteem by being force-fed a diet intended instead to produce self-doubt. Self-esteem is revered on Earth, but only in books. Much lip service is paid to self-worth, but it is seldom reinforced or even encouraged. You believe that by discouraging self-confidence in the young you will help them to grow into confident adults. It is a mystery, but I think I have a handle on it."

"Go on," I almost begged.

"You tell young people to learn to think for themselves, but you rarely allow them to do it. Instead you provide them with an education that discourages decision making at every turn. You give them lessons on becoming self-confident and then take away the very experiences that would lead to that end. All day and all night in their homes your television programs show them how to pursue the exact opposite of self-esteem.''

''What do you mean 'the exact opposite'?''

''You tell them that sex appeal can be purchased by wearing the right bluejeans, or by using a bottle of expensive perfume. You show them pictures all the time, of women acting like dolts, trying to please their men, jiggling their bodies for attention, wearing the proper artificial fragrances and getting the desired results, that is, approving looks from men; or women who cannot contain themselves because a man smokes a particular brand of cigarette or wears a specific after-shave lotion. Then you expect them to grow into self-confident adults.''

''But self-esteem isn't discouraged on all fronts,'' I protested.

''Maybe not, but the overwhelming emphasis seems to be on teaching obedience rather than responsible thinking, on fitting in and conforming rather than being independent and creative. You make being an independent thinker extremely difficult, particularly for young people.''

''But I saw a great deal of dependency and conformity on Uranus. Why do you find it so disconcerting when you see it here?'' I asked.

''Once again you forget our separate realities. On Uranus we have the dependency diodes that we discussed in depth. Furthermore with self-rejection lotion as a necessary part of our existence, we simply have no voice in the matter. But it's not like that here on Earth at all.''

I had forgotten about our separate realities. She was tied into those real-world exigencies, and I didn't want her to go through that salt water/fresh water analogy that had made so much sense earlier. "You are correct, Eykis," I replied. "Please go on."

"I can't figure out why so many of you resist independent thinking and new ideas, when progress is impossible without them. You make such a big thing about progress and then do everything possible to stand in the way of the only people who can bring it about—those who think for themselves and aren't afraid of new ideas."

"Don't you think young people need discipline? Shouldn't they learn to respect their elders and how to get along in life?" I asked.

"The Earthling behaviors I'm describing have nothing to do with respect. You can't respect anyone else if you don't respect yourself. Or to put it more logically, on Earth your reality dictates that you can't give away what you don't have. Moreover, you can never grow into a self-respecting adult if you are learning to conform and fit in. If you are just like everybody else, then what do you have to offer?" she asked without expecting an answer. "If you want young people to be disciplined, you must teach them from the earliest moments of their lives to become their own parents. If you want them to just get along, as you put it, then they'll have no sense of purpose in their lives, because that only comes from getting along with yourself, not trying to please everyone else. Finally, the idea of respecting your elders makes no more sense than the reverse, that is, respecting your juniors. Respect is earned, and being older or younger is not relevant.''

"So what is your discovery, then?" I asked Eykis.

"I think I know why all of you seem so determined to teach self-rejection. It's not because you don't have any of the self-rejection lotion we use on Uranus. I think you do it to insure employment. I just can't find any other reason.''

"Employment! How can reinforcing self-rejection have anything to do with employment?" I asked.

"Designer jeans, perfumes with fraudulent claims of sex appeal in a bottle, sprays for your breath, and soaps to win approval all have to be invented, manufactured, sold, inventoried, demonstrated, and advertised through an entire chain of specialized job titles. Similarly, all those social workers, therapists of every description, clerks and bureaucrats who keep the social services working are also being paid to do so. The endless array of aspirin, tranquilizers, and medicine of every description to treat those afflicted with poor self-images also contribute a great deal to this economic plan.''

She could have gone on with many more examples, but I interrupted. "You sound as if it's a conspiracy to keep people neurotic in order to maintain the economy," I stated.

"That's what I find confusing," she replied, unaffected by my use of the word conspiracy. "Neurosis keeps your system alive. When people think like conformists, they all go out and buy the 'right' things so they can be just like everyone else. It helps the economy when people are convinced that they can purchase sex appeal, and many, many people benefit when dependency and self-depreciation are encouraged.''

She was really convinced of the veracity of her theory.

''I find it hard to dispute,'' I said. ''But I don't really believe it represents any deliberate effort. It may appear that way, but I don't think it was ever intended as a ruse to keep employment levels up.''

''Whether or not it's deliberate is irrelevant. It is what is. The rewards for conformity are omnipresent, be it Asia, Africa, Europe, or North America. People are told how to think in the name of obedience. It doesn't matter whether it's obedience to the state, your teachers, a business, or even your parents, the end results are the same. Those with little or no confidence in themselves, and no innovative ideas, become servants to those who give the orders. Then those in charge, who are equally afflicted with self-doubt, conspire to create an entire society of unhappy conformists.''

She told me about people she had seen or read about, who victimized others and defended their actions with ''It's only my job,'' or some such easy excuse. She pounded her fist on the table again, saying, ''People who have been encouraged to be independent rather than conformist in their thinking couldn't possibly do anything horrible to another person in the name of 'doing a job' or 'everybody else does it,' could they? So you create jobs of conformism and the system works,'' she said, answering her own question. ''But maybe we can end that,'' she said, almost under her breath. She had apparently been giving some thought to the gifts she had alluded to earlier.

"For the life of me," she said after a few moments, "I still can't see why you react to your reality so unrealistically. Many of you even get sick for no real reason connected to reality. Many of you are fatigued and even old and senile for reasons that escape my powers of perception. Let's stop for now," she said. "I do have something else I want to discuss with you."

"Yes, yes," I encouraged her. "You've mentioned a proposal or a gift to Earth of some sort. I'm willing to do anything you ask of me."

"As of now, we must stop thinking about what isn't working and why. In the little time left we must direct our thoughts and energy to solutions. Ways to make my proposal work. I'll think more about it tonight, and tomorrow we can go over it together."

I had no idea what she had in mind. She had talked repeatedly about thinking in terms of solutions rather than problems, and I'm sure our rather lengthy discussions of the past two days had helped her organize her thoughts. She saw our problems and understood how we thought, felt, and conducted ourselves.

What could she offer an entire planet? As we parted for the night, my love for her was rekindled. I began to think about her leaving in a few days, and I had to send these thoughts away. The idea of never seeing her again was painful, and I didn't want to corrode this moment with my anguished thoughts. Besides, I laughed to myself, I'll connect the worry-wares to the appropriate terminals and change them. As she left, it occurred to me that we had spent almost the entire day in a little picnic cove on a hard bench, and I'd never noticed a moment of discomfort. As she walked away I was sure I could hear her muttering over and over what she'd said so clearly a few moments earlier: "Why do they react so unrealistically to their reality? We can fix that, if they'll allow it."

6 · Eykis' Proposal

I'd spent the night tossing in my bed with my mind working overtime. I didn't want to waste precious moments sleeping. My life had been deeply touched by this remarkable woman. She was a guru of sorts. Not the kind before whom one kneels in search of the unrevealed. In fact, she was quite the opposite. She was a saint of common sense, asking you in terse, objective language just to take off your dark glasses and see for yourself what you've allowed to become murky in your life.

Her clear logic and wonderfully sensible observations made me look at myself and my world with new eyes, eyes that were now focused, without the myopia of customs and habitual thought. She was awakening me: me, a person who had prided himself on his "conscious posture" all his life. I was now much more aware of how much I'd taken for granted as simply the way we think here on Earth. I was beginning to challenge what had previously been considered "only natural" a few days ago. My mind was spinning with new thoughts and ways to convey what I'd begun to learn from Eykis. As I finally drifted off to sleep, I wondered what gifts this remarkable woman would offer tomorrow morning.

"What would you say to an entirely new way of thinking?" Eykis asked, as her first inquiry the next morning in the coffee shop where we had agreed to meet.

"What do you mean, *entirely new way of thinking?*"

"I mean, suppose I could provide the people of Earth, all of them, with an entirely new way of perceiving their reality? I'm talking about the greatest gift imaginable. The opportunity to tune in directly to their own reality in such a way that virtually all the so-called problems you face would be eliminated."

"But how? In what way?" I asked excitedly.

"I've been giving this a great amount of Uranus-like thought," she began, almost repeating my Earthlike thought of the moment.

"Almost all your problems stem from the way you teach your children to think. If you're ever going to achieve true evolution as a people, you must somehow break the 'thinking chain' that keeps you in 'behavioral bonds.' I think I might be able to provide your people with an opportunity for direct contact with me and my unique reality-only approach to thinking. That alone might enable your people to turn Earth into the place it was designed to become."

"How can you know what Earth was designed tc

become?'' I asked, only for the purpose of having her continue with her proposal.

"I can only consider what my home would be like if we were not bridled by our own reality. We on Uranus are not self-destructive or neurotic without positive purpose. It is our reality that makes us what we are. If your choices were available there, the possibilities for creative living and fulfillment would be staggering. Since it is clearly impossible for me single-handedly to alter my reality system, perhaps I can instead offer your people the benefit of learning to live happily and comfortably within your own.''

"But aren't we altering our own reality system by not living within it?''

"Of course not,'' she said, brushing off my distraction. "You on Earth are still living each day within your own reality system. That is a condition of your existence. But you're deluding yourselves by thinking in ways which have little to do with that very same reality. It's as if you don't like what exists, so you invent new thinking modes to help you pretend that life is what you want it to be, rather than what it is.''

I agreed with her, but sometimes it took me a few moments of mental gymnastics to understand why I agreed. "All right, so *reality just is,* and we aren't being realistic when we create ways to pretend that it is any other way.''

"True,'' she replied, "but I think we might be able to put some dents in the armor. Would you be willing to help me set it up?''

"I'll do everything I can—anything at all,'' I insisted.

"Terrific. Here's what I have in mind: I'd like to call together representatives of the top leadership of various fields of human activity. Please inform your government of my presence here, and arrange an all-day meeting, with representatives from various segments of your world society. I'll introduce myself to these people, and tell them about myself and our visits together. I'll explain how we spent our time together on Uranus and what you discovered, how I came to accompany you back to Earth, and how I have observed your world culture incognito. Each of the representatives attending the gathering will be able to question me. My reality-only orientation will prevent me from distorting what I've seen, and I would provide the representatives with genuinely truthful answers to their questions. Since I'm incapable of telling them anything but what is, they'll be able to put the results of this day-long conference to work. You will have the greatest gifts that I can leave for you. And leave you I must, in just a few days."

I was thrilled at the notion of a reality conference peopled by representatives of a variety of human enterprises. "But what if the governments refuse to participate, what if they elect to appoint a series of committees to study your proposal, or to study you through the use of lie detectors, legislative inquiries, psychiatric analysis, and on and on, which is the way we do things here? They'd put you in a prison or a zoo and investigate you to death," I said.

"That's *your* job," she stated, seemingly unconcerned about my obsession with Earthly red tape. "You must explain that these methodological options are unavailable to them. You and I know that I can return to Uranus at will, despite any Earthly protests to the contrary. You know that I am incapable of studying a problem in a committee. That I am only able to work on solutions and unable to focus on what *hasn't been done,* or *shouldn't be done*. I am always focused on DOING. You'll have to become one of the humans in the first of the three categories I have observed."

"What three categories?" I asked. I hadn't heard her mention them prior to this moment.

"I'm sorry, I thought I had spelled them out to you. In all my research I discovered three kinds of human beings on Earth: those who say, 'Let's make it happen'; those who say, 'It can't happen'; and the largest category, those who say, 'What happened?' You are simply going to have to get into category one and make it happen. You'll have to explain the zero-option to the representatives. You can give them the evidence you have, lay your cards on the table, and then we'll have a conference on Saturday, which will be just before I leave for Uranus. I will leave on schedule regardless of what happens. If the representatives refuse the things I have to offer, I'll give them to you to distribute as you wish. This is my proposal. It is intended to help the people of Earth change their thinking so they can improve their world and make it really work for everyone. Thinking is the basis for every single major and minor difficulty you encounter. The problems that arise in politics, religion, education, families, business, the military, society, medicine, and every form of human enterprise are due to self-programed unreal thinking. At least I can try to leave you with a new format for thinking that could ultimately put an end to the problems that have plagued your people throughout the ages. Do you think you can arrange it?"

"Well, to be honest, I'm not sure it's as simple as you think it is to bypass the hugely convoluted bureaucracy that would be involved in such an undertaking. You see, on Earth we prefer to study rather than tackle a problem. This is particularly true at the leadership levels. But I'll damn sure try, and if I encounter the kind of resistance that I'm accustomed to, I can take matters into my own hands and stand in for the world leaders myself. It would take some research, but I could do it in the next few days, and then I could film your responses. In either case, I love your proposal, Eykis, and I'll see that it gets to our people in whatever fashion I can figure out. Will that suffice?" I asked, hoping she wouldn't be upset because of my realistic assessment of how our world's leaders would respond to her offer.

"I love it!" she said, surprising me with her willingness to allow me to even suggest altering her proposal. "Let's do it your way. It will save incalculable hours of persuasion on your part, and you'll have the reality-only answers in permanent form, which you can use in whatever way you can work out. You'll have only two days to gather the questions, and you must keep them aligned to what the various leaders would want to know, rather than having them colored by your own perceptions based on the time we've spent together. You understand, the essence of this filmed inquiry must be thinking. We're not trying to destroy any institutions or pass judgment on any of Earth's physical realities. Remember, they are absolutely perfect, and remember also that, except for a few minor differences, they duplicate my Uranus reality. What we want to focus on is the inner world of thinking and attitudes that lead to, as you call them, problems.''

"But what precisely is it about the inner thinking and attitudes of Earth that I'm to focus on during our final session? I've only heard that we are 'wrong' when we think in self-destructive or neurotic ways. While I admit that you've given me plenty of examples of the incorrect thinking of neurotics, I need to know the components of our thinking in order to simulate questions and responses of leaders in all walks of life." I was looking for guidelines to help me with my homework. True to her character, Eykis provided me with a blueprint that would enable me to go about my task in the most effective and challenging way possible.

"In addition to being 'incorrect,' much of your Earthly thinking is out of focus. Consequently you have blurred thinking, which leads to the ultimate in self-destructive thought."

"In what areas is the *out-of-focus* element most obvious? How does it reveal itself?"

"So much of the Earthly way of thinking leads to an illusion of happiness which remains throughout an entire lifetime. For example, most people are satisfied with appearances and size as substitutes for quality in their attitudes, feelings, and behavior. There is no possibility for happiness in these appearances that people pursue so vigorously, because happiness is an inner activity. Do you see what I mean by unfocused thinking?"

"But how does pursuing appearances rather than quality lead to being wrong?" I asked.

"People who direct life toward appearances are focusing on how their possessions appear to others. They give up their sense of satisfaction in what they are doing, for future satisfaction that can never arrive. They are obsessed with how others view their objects, or they actually look for happiness from their objects. These are both dead ends, because happiness is a strictly human venture that can only be experienced internally. Neither the size of your possessions nor the praise you receive for their appearance can provide any sense of happiness or fulfillment. Consequently those who seek appearances of any kind with the hope of achieving happiness are just plain wrong."

"And you think that *quality* in one's thinking can lead to happiness?" I asked.

"Well, first please understand that there is no way *to* happiness. Happiness *is* the way. And happiness is how you decide to think in each moment of your life. When you're thinking happiness, you are happy, regardless of what you are doing, or what your reality is at the moment."

"So you think you can be happy any time, regardless of the conditions of your life at the moment?" I asked.

"Of course! You can choose *happiness thinking* any time, and that is precisely what happiness is. I'm not asking people to pretend they're happy when they're not. I simply think that since you on Earth can always choose how you will think at any moment, you can refocus your thinking by emphasizing the quality of an experience, rather than how the experience appears to you or to others. Furthermore, you can see that the objects you collect can never provide happiness. Not on Earth, in terms of your own reality.''

"So you would have us teach quality thinking versus appearance thinking?'' I wondered aloud to Eykis.

"I'm only saying that appearance thinking leads to wrong thinking, which can and does have disastrous effects at all levels of your culture. Training people in terms of quality from the time they are very young would help to create future generations of quality-rather than appearance-oriented people.''

"But how could we do that in our profit-oriented business world?'' I wondered, beginning to protest the simplicity of such thinking.

"Be sure to bring that up on Saturday,'' she said, gently reminding me of our rendezvous.

"You said there were other blurry thinking concepts that led to the rampant 'wrongness' of thought we have here.''

"Yes, of course. In place of *ethical* thinking, you seem to emphasize 'rules thinking,' and you encourage your youngsters to do the same.''

"Ethics versus rules?'' I repeated.

"Yes. A rules thinker is one who does what he is told, regardless of the situation,'' she offered bluntly.

"But we need rules,'' I protested. "Without them all of society would collapse. For example, it is a rule to stop at a red traffic light. Imagine if people ignored it."

"Why do you stop at a red traffic light?" she asked.

"Because it's against the law, and besides, I'd likely get a ticket or, even worse, have an accident," I shot back.

"You mean that if new laws were passed tomorrow, making it legal to go through red traffic lights, you would then go through them?" she questioned.

"Eh?" was all I was able to say.

"The real reason why you don't go through red traffic lights is that it is unethical to do so. Placing your life or the lives of others in jeopardy is plainly unethical," she said.

"But we need to go beyond merely talking about traffic rules."

"Red lights in traffic was your choice for an example, not mine," she reminded me. "Besides, we can save this for Saturday as well. I'm sure your governmental and educational specialists will have much to say about the need for rules-oriented thinking."

I jotted this down as a reminder for my research.

"Rules-oriented thinking places the responsibility for behavior on the rule, rather than the individual. When rules, laws, and policies are held accountable as the cause of human thinking, ethics must take a back seat. When people base their behavior on what others tell them is correct, ethical thinking is almost impossible and the opportunity for fulfillment and happiness is stifled once again," she said.

"In what ways?" I asked.

"You even have 'happy hours' here on Earth!

Meaning, I suppose, that other hours can't be. You need a rule to tell you when you can be happy and a supply of cheap booze to insure the result. Once again, happiness is an inner experience, rules are outer experiences. Ethics, on the other hand, are inner rules which never allow a person to behave in a way that would be *harmful* to others."

When we first met, Eykis hadn't even known the word "harmful." Now she knew it all too well.

"So ethical-thinking training would teach people how to think for themselves?"

"Yes, if it were based on real ethics. The need for so many rules for almost every facet of your lives would be eliminated. You have rules for virtually everything, including when you can have a beer, what God will do to you if you're not obeying the laws, and even what courses you must take in school. Tell me, please, how can people learn to become decision makers if all decisions are already made for them by the rules and policies that you seem to rely upon so heavily?" she asked.

I did what I always did when I couldn't give her a sensible answer. I answered her question with a question.

I said, "That's two. Quality in place of appearance, and ethics in place of rules. Any more?"

"Yes, my friend. I've noticed that most of the people on Earth substitute domination for personal integrity or *authority* in their thinking," she said.

"How do domination and authority thinking differ, and how do they lead to this global picture of our wrongness?" I asked.

"Quite simply," she replied. "Domination thinking involves victimizing or controlling others. Much of the thinking I've noted is directed toward the subjugation of others, whether it's nation subjugating nation, parents their offspring, or spouses each other. There is almost a universal obsession here with attempts to control and dominate. When thinking is directed at seeing how much one can control others, it cannot be focused on personal happiness and self-direction. Since we've already established that happiness is an inner concept, then outer or domination thinking ultimately leads to the wrong conclusion: 'If only I can get the people around me to be as I want them to be, or even as I am, then I'll be powerful and, consequently, happy.'"

"So what constitutes 'authority' or 'integrity' thinking, as you put it?" I asked.

"It's quite the opposite," she retorted. "It is an inner rather than an outer concept. A person devoted to increasing his authority over himself, to becoming more personally masterful, to being able to share his mastery with others, is not asking to dominate anyone. Such a person is using his thought processes just to *be*, and to allow those around him to do the same. He does not interfere in anyone else's life. He tries only to learn from others rather than control or manipulate them. This is integrity thinking, and a person who practices it has no need to seek authority by dominating others. He has it automatically. Those who seek authority through domination demonstrate their own lack of the very quality they seek to prove they possess," she replied.

"But what about our enemies, those who would seek to dominate us? Don't we have to show them that we refuse to be dominated?" I asked.

"Again it is your domination style of thinking which leads you to ask this. I am thinking *globally*. I am not talking to 'you' as opposed to 'them.' All people must be educated to think in personal integrity ways, and ultimately end the concept of enemy once and for all. As long as you think in we/they terms, you will be able to blame the enemy for your thoughts of dominance. But again, save this for Saturday. I'm quite sure it will surface many times," she said. "There are two additional areas of myopic thought which you need to be aware of as you prepare your Saturday agenda, even though they overlap somewhat with the three I've just described. Most people on your planet practice 'achievement thinking,' as opposed to '*knowledge* thinking.' As a result many people on Earth are wrong and ultimately neurotic and unfulfilled.

"People on Earth don't accept the kind of thinking that allows for knowledge for the sake of knowledge. They see little use for knowledge that doesn't lead to achievement. Hence you see the ultimate folly of students actually purchasing credits and notations on a transcript, regardless of whether any knowledge of the subject matter is retained. Achievement seems to be the reason for thinking, and it is another dead-end pursuit."

"Because?" I interrupted, just to let her know I was with her.

"Because achievements are external and happiness is internal. An A on a transcript and an understanding of a poem are not even related in reality, and yet most people study poetry for the grade. The use of a poem that is understood cannot be stated in achievement terminology, nor can the money earned from the mastery of Marketing 101, although this logic escapes most Earthlings and also contributes to their unhappiness. Knowledge thinking says that anything you learn can benefit you and enrich your life. Achievement thinking says that you must be able to measure, weigh, or spend what you study and that it will be manifested later when the fruits of your study of behavior are to be picked. But if it fails to arrive later—and on Earth it never does, because you only get NOW—then your achievement thinking was all for naught. With knowledge thinking for the pure joy of knowledge itself and all that it offers, one can never be unhappy or disappointed because the thinking, feeling, and behavior themselves are the inner rewards. I hope we can help your people to begin to shift from achievement thinking to knowledge thinking.''

''But then won't our great achievements begin to subside?'' I asked.

''In fact, people chasing achievement are destined to be unfulfilled. And this in fact inhibits their achievements, the very things they so desperately seek. But let's save this also. There'll be many questions on this one, I can guarantee it. I suspect it is the most widespread kind of wrong thinking on your planet.''

''You mentioned one additional element of our fuzzy thinking that leads to our wrong conclusions,'' I said.

''Yes, it's a summary of the above four. In place of

serenity and inner-peace thinking, it seems to me that people on Earth are consumed with acquisitions. Inner-serenity thinking is hardly taught anywhere on your planet, with the possible exception of some Far Eastern cults that are largely scoffed at by most of your people. And yet inner-serenity thinking is the complete key available to virtually everyone on your planet. Physical and mental illnesses are almost non-existent when a person learns to think in inner-serenity ways. Your highest achievers, your most fulfilled people, your most innovative minds in all fields seem to share this inner-peace thinking, and yet so few emulate it. Instead, they substitute for it the pursuit of things, achievements, awards, trophies, or the approval of others. If my gift to your people is to have any significance, it must help them to transform this kind of thinking. It is necessary to cross over from seeking acquisitions to achieving inner perfection. When you reach the goal of a serene feeling of wholeness, you will find acquisitions will be in amounts sufficient to reinforce the serenity. People must stop going at it backward by trying to make acquisitions bring about serenity. To put it simply, it is impossible, because the thinking is wrong. I'll see you Saturday morning, right here. Bring your questions and prepare to represent your various roles. Ask what you wish. I'll speak only as I know how. That is, *The Truth,* as seen by Eykis of Uranus.''

I wrote down the five fuzzy-thinking categories:

Quality instead of Appearance thinking.
Ethics instead of Rules thinking.

Knowledge instead of Achievement thinking.
Integrity instead of Domination thinking.
Serenity instead of Acquisitions thinking.

Then I hurried away with my notes and tapes stuffed into my briefcase. Saturday was less than forty-eight hours away. I suspected that I was about to participate in bestowing the greatest gifts ever received by mankind. I wondered also if we would ever even unwrap them. But as Eykis would say, knowledge thinking would lead to achievement by accident. At least we would have the knowledge. I knew I couldn't ask for more.

• Part Three •

EYKIS' GIFTS

7 · Reality-Only Conversations

I settled into my task with the full realization of what I wanted to accomplish, and how precious little time was available. My objective was clear. I was to provide Eykis with a forum in which she would be able to offer her specialized wisdom to everyone on Earth. I could not let this unique opportunity pass without tapping her reality-only brain to the maximum. She had seen what she could offer us and she didn't take any special credit for her abilities. She was simply incapable of using her mind in any way that conflicted with reality. Now she was on Earth, millions of miles from her own home, willing to give us the benefit of her atypical self.

I wanted to invite every single leader in every field of human endeavor to sit and talk with her. The benefits to mankind would be incalculable. In just over a week, she had transformed my thinking. I was a better, happier human being for having known her, and an infinitely more wise and sensible person for having actually spent time in direct conversation with her. I glowed with the intoxication that comes from anticipating a peak experience. In this case, it was the prospect of exposing influential people to Eykis' remarkable mind. But I also knew fully the reality that she was presenting. We had one day in which to complete the gifts she was offering. She absolutely refused to put up with any hassles or cumbersome bureaucratic snags. She was definitely not interested in being judged or in participating in any silly arguments with narrow-minded disbelievers and she would not engage in any senseless bickering. I had quickly learned that when Eykis made a point, she would not continue in endless rehashing as a means of communicating. She simply expressed what she observed, stated it in honest, nonjudgmental language, and then, when I still wanted to argue, she would unceremoniously stop. With Eykis there was no haranguing, no emotional pleas, and, most emphatically, no quibbling with illogical thinking.

We had discussed the ground rules for Saturday's simulated press conference. The number of participants would be limited to representatives of the highest level of thinkers and leaders in five different fields of human activity. Each representative would be allotted thirty minutes to ask or discuss anything that interested him. Eykis would answer any and all questions. There would be no restrictions, no limits. Each participant could choose either to interact with Eykis or to just ask questions, and I was to arrange for eight full hours of filming to record every word of each conversation or interview. At the end, Eykis would address herself to any subjects of interest to the entire group. Then, by way of closing, she would offer to everyone what she called the Secrets of the Universe. These so-called secrets would be her final gift to us, and while she had referred to them on several occasions during our discussions, I still did not know what they would involve.

The most challenging thing for me was my own level of participation. I was to assume the roles of the five leaders as if I were actually living in each person's mind and body. I wasted no time. I spent the next two days preparing myself for the Saturday press conference. The thought of what this film could do for our planet and its inhabitants was staggering. At the same time I was frightened. Eykis' thinking was profound in its simplicity. She might be dismissed as a simpleton. But that was not for me to "worry" about. Virtually every transcendent thinker and creative person who has ever lived has been viewed by his contemporaries as too simple. It seemed that all great minds I had ever read about had encountered constant opposition from mediocre thinkers. Even if the whole world ignored Eykis' gifts now, perhaps someday it would appreciate her. Jesus was scorned in his time, and the Greeks forced Socrates to drink poison because he talked too much (and that from the people who invented democracy). There was no more time for wondering how she would be received. I had to prepare myself to make sure she could give us all she wanted to. We would leave the judging to the critics.

As I worked at my questions, I recalled that Eykis

hadn't cared to know which role I would be playing, nor even when I would be shifting from one to another. She had said to me, "I don't need to prepare to be myself. You'll be recording Eykis' truths on Saturday. Do whatever you wish, ask what you desire, use any format or none at all. Let's just do it."

Eykis arrived early on Saturday morning. She appeared to be wonderfully alive and eager to begin.

"You look prepared," she said. "If you have everything in order, let's begin. We'll keep this informal and enjoyable for both of us."

She was reassuring, obviously trying to help me relax, since I was a beehive of activity. "Almost everything is set. It's wonderful to see you today. I missed you terribly these past two days, but I was so busy thinking and preparing myself for this that the time flew by," I said. She gave me that quizzical look that I had come to understand. I was sure she didn't really comprehend what "I missed you" meant, since it was at that moment that she looked puzzled. However, she had also learned to avoid asking me to explain these kinds of thoughts, since she had been here among Earthlings for some time and had accustomed herself to our strange ways. On Uranus, people didn't choose to miss each other when they were temporarily separated. They preferred to deal with the present moment and they didn't evaluate love on the unreal basis of "missing each other." She had talked to me about this before, explaining in depth how this plugging into the now was accomplished on Uranus. She was totally absorbed in this moment.

"We're going to be talking about religion first. I

have several questions to ask you about the way we practice religion here on Earth, but before I get to that, I would like to find out about religion on Uranus and in your own personal life," I said, attempting to lose myself in this role with all of the fervor of a religious leader.

"What would you like to know about me and religion?" she asked.

"Well, first, are you a religious person?"

"Yes, I think of myself as very religious," she responded instantly.

"Do you believe in a supreme being, a creator of the universe?"

"I think it's quite possible, although I can't honestly say I believe it. I don't know. None of us on Uranus do. But it certainly is possible. I don't concern myself with believing it or not. I appreciate my planet and the universe, and I live within it as morally as I know how. I'm not preoccupied with how it started, but rather in enjoying it and making it a better place for everyone," she responded.

"How do you know what is moral, if you don't believe in the existence of God?" I said.

"When I say I don't believe, I don't at all discount the possibility of the existence of God. It is quite possible, indeed quite probable, and I am totally open to it. I simply don't know. Therefore I don't use words like 'believe' as you do. Second, morality is well defined on Uranus. It is not a religious affair at all," she said.

"How is your morality defined?"

"Quite simply, any behavior that doesn't interfere

with another individual's right to live as he would like
to is moral," she responded.

"But how can you say that when you talk about
feeling-hurters, guilt-prodders, and the like?"

"That is our reality, it is out of our hands and has
nothing to do with morality. Just as your DC-10s and
Skylabs are your reality. You know how to produce
them and you do, despite the fact that there are casualties associated with these realities. You do not judge
them, nor the people who invent, manufacture, and fly
the aircraft, immoral. Once they are a part of your
reality they cannot be sent away by simple fiat. They
exist because the knowledge to create them exists.
Feeling-hurters are a part of our reality and that is
that. On Uranus hurt feelings are not judged as *bad,*
they are a condition of our reality. It would be like
saying that sharks are immoral because they eat min-
nows. That is their reality and should not be confused
with morality," she said.

"How can you know what is right and wrong if you
don't have religion to assist you?" I asked.

"Morality has nothing to do with right and wrong,
it is as I defined it just a moment ago. Moreover, right
and wrong do not exist independently of man's willingness to apply these labels on Earth," she shot
back.

"But we do have right and wrong," I protested as I
believed my religious leader would point out, adding,
"and someone has to uphold these standards."

"You do have people, religious people and others,
defining right and wrong here, but that doesn't mean
they exist."

"But killing, for example, is wrong," I suggested.

"Except when you declare wars on each other, then it is right and moral," she said with no evidence of malice.

"But war is an exception," I said.

"Then so is saying that killing is wrong," she answered. "Here on Earth there is no morality outside of man's definition of it for his own convenience. It is that way today, and it has been that way throughout your recorded history."

"Where would you suggest that we go to help people to be more moral by your definition?" I asked.

"To the only place people on Earth can go, and that is to themselves. You can train people to think more ethically rather than by rules. Blind obedience to rules and laws just because they are affiliated with a religious sect can and does lead to outrageously immoral acts," she replied.

"Such as?"

"Such as wars in the name of religion in Ireland, Iran, Iraq, Syria, and all over your world. Killing in the name of religion is still killing, even though you call it patriotism or religious duty. Were you to train each other, especially your young people, to think ethically, you would never resort to killing for *any* reason. Consequently you would raise moral standards by helping individuals think for themselves in ethical self-determining ways. A human being who believed in morality would never make a decision to kill if he or she considered killing immoral. And if every individual used his or her own mind and conscience to determine a personal moral position on killing, there would be no one to do the killing, and no one to order it either," she said emphatically.

"But isn't it unrealistic to imagine that everyone would be moral under those conditions?" I asked.

"Morality is an individual matter, not an *everyone* matter. When you teach and practice not to kill throughout your world, you will have individuals deciding not to kill. Only then will you have morality. Regardless of how much rhetoric you spout to the contrary, there is no *right* and *wrong* on your planet. You only have individuals applying these labels. It should be the role of a religious moral leader to foster nonkilling behavior, rather than comfort those in military war zones. Your churches should be outraged at any violation of morality and not participate in affronts by condemning them only with lip service."

"Well, would you have people on Earth believe in God?"

"They are free to do so as they choose. However, I would tell them to stop asking God to do what they have the power to do themselves."

"Why do people here ask God to do that?" I asked.

"Because people on your planet are afraid to *be* God. They want someone else to do it for them. They use prayer as a means for communicating with God, and virtually all the prayer I've observed is a plea for God to make the world into something other than what it is."

"How?" I asked.

"Listen to your prayers. 'Please God, make my troubles go away.' 'Please God, help my family.' 'Please God, help us win this football game.' These are the pleas of people who want God to do things for them.''

''How would you alter that prayer, Eykis?''

''I would look within myself for the strength to help me alleviate suffering in the world. I'd ask myself to push harder, to go the extra step, to stop whining, to accept the world as it is. If I wanted to give God the credit for giving me free will, terrific, but I'd want to remind myself precisely what free will entails. It has nothing to do with asking God to do something for me,'' she responded.

''So you believe that we have made God into an external concept to which we give either credit or blame,'' I summarized.

''You've not only made God into an external concept, you've turned all of religion into precisely what you have just described. You even measure how religious your people are by such unrelated behavior as their attendance at church, recitation of scriptures that are not understood, whether they practice birth control, the symbols they worship, and so on. I even heard a man explaining to his friend how happy he was that he was going to attend mass on Saturday evening rather than Sunday morning, so that he could 'get it over with.' Getting religious services *over with* is not a healthy signal when you are trying to cultivate individual integrity and morality. In fact, it is precisely the opposite of what it was originally intended to accomplish.''

''How is it the opposite?'' I asked.

''What you have done with religion on your planet is to completely turn around what started out as an opportunity to help mankind to look inward and by so doing develop personal standards of conduct that would make the world a better place. Religion has become a catechism of guilt, worry, fear, anxiety. As you know, I see this as elementary incorrect thinking. Man has used religious affiliation to act out his own wrong, self-destructive, power-hungry thinking, and then called the conforming behavior that follows such dogma 'religion.' Your religious colleagues have almost constantly used the name of God for immoral ends. You can't read a newspaper anywhere on your planet without seeing the evidence. You see wars and executions in the name of God! You see murder and stealing, skyjacking and terrorism, all in the name of God!'' she exclaimed.

''But those are zealots, fanatics,'' I protested. ''Not all religion condones such activity.''

''It just depends on who is doing the name calling,'' she reminded me. ''In your wars you have priests, ministers, mullahs, and rabbis praying to help you kill more of the enemy. Those on one side exhort their followers to regard all others as immoral. I'm not talking exclusively about wars, either. When you tell young people, 'This is what God wants you to do,' or 'You'll go to hell if you don't attend church,' or 'Please God as WE think God wants you to please her,' then you're still taking away that free will. Anything which encourages people to act in blind obedience to unquestioned authority is an invitation to fit in and behave as they are told by God's self-anointed representatives. When external behavior turns into 'good,' you label it religious and applaud it, and when it leads to wars, blind obedience, stealing, or anything else, you overlook it, call it a necessary exception, or punish it, depending upon how conveniently it fits into your externally imposed dogma."

"But don't you think you're being too hard on religion? Certainly you must think it serves a purpose in our world," I said hopefully.

"Keep in mind," she gently reminded me, "I am only capable of relating what is, I can't say what you would like me to say because it would make you and your colleagues happier. But, of course, religion can, and in some cases does, provide a wonderful service to humanity."

"What do you see as the benefits of religion on Earth?"

"It provides people with an arena for self-examination. It provides stimulation for the soul and helps people examine their life choices. It helps them see how they can improve the quality of life on Earth. Religion can be an avenue for human expression that encourages self-development and appreciation for the beauty of your marvelous universe," she said without pausing.

"But you don't feel that it provides this as often as it might?" I summarized.

"I've seen it only rarely. For the most part, religion has been used as a tool for furthering man's selfish lust for power and control over others. Many of the most inhumane acts ever recorded on your planet were carried out with God or religion as the rationale," she said.

"How would you use religion, as you've seen it on

Earth, in the most propitious manner?'' I asked, recognizing that I had already spent a great deal of time on this one area, and I still had many more hats to try on with Eykis before this day and her visit were complete.

"Instead of forcing people to practice religion that tells them how to think, encourage them to think for themselves. That is the most religiously freeing experience possible on Earth. Rather than imposing rules, laws, and dogma on your parishioners, you should be asking them to begin taking moral responsibility for their own lives. Instead of measuring religious behavior in terms of external symbols, I would measure it by how well each person is able to realize his own potential for individual morality. If this goal was ever achieved—and where else but in religious teachings are you better equipped to take on the task?—then all of the terrible immoral calamities you've brought about on your planet, such as war, crime, starvation, and pollution, would become obsolete.

"From what I, Eykis, can see, you have that option, unlike us on Uranus. We have a reality system that often precludes our having individual free will. But you, you can think as you elect to, and that is a gift each of you is misusing. All too often, in the religious institutions you so proudly erect, you do all you can to rid your people of their individual morality, while proclaiming quite the opposite in your religious rhetoric,'' she concluded.

"So you would move religion, in all forms, from the external to the internal side?" I asked, wanting to be certain that I had recorded her statement properly.

"Yes, but you needn't take my word for it. Look to the teachings of one of your most famous religious leaders, who spelled it out in black and white for you."

"To whom do you refer?"

"When the admirers of Jesus, like most disciples today of all religions, asked, 'Where do we find the kingdom of heaven? How do we get there?' he replied with one sentence that communicates all I've said here this morning: 'Don't look outside yourself for it, *the kingdom of heaven is within.*' That's the message. It isn't a place you arrive at as a reward for being just like everybody else, or doing what you're told. It is within. That is precisely what I meant when I said earlier that people are afraid to BE God. God must reside within each person. People should look at their own capacity for greatness and seek out the strength to do it themselves. BEING God is not disrespectful in the least. It involves putting total responsibility for morality on your own shoulders, and using the free will that is your birthright on Earth. I am sad to say that I've seen very little evidence on Earth that anyone even remotely connected to any religion understands the simple little secret of the universe that Jesus unveiled two thousand years ago—the kingdom of heaven is within."

Even after many hours with Eykis, I found her simple honesty amazing. She stated her beliefs without any of the usual caution that typifies nearly all discussions on Earth. She related only what she perceived to be true. She knew nothing of such things as duplicity, exaggeration, or couching truths in more palatable language. Even so, I was anxious to change topics. While I enjoyed playing the role of religious representative, I was also squirming a bit under Eykis' straightforward responses. Religion is one of those areas that is so loaded with emotion for most of us, that it seemed strange to hear her talk without even so much as a twinge of fear of retribution. She wasn't at all concerned with how she would be perceived. She cared nothing for her ratings. She was being Eykis, sharing her own truths in the form of observations she had made. Nothing more! I was loving it and her.

"As a person representing the realistic world of business," I asked her, starting into my second role, "just what are your thoughts about such things as profits, money, and production?" I had given her no warning as to where I was headed.

"I see that it is possible to live happily and fully with or without profits and money on your planet. I feel that working for money itself is self-defeating because it teaches that acquisitions, achievement, and appearances are the reasons for working. These things can never bring about complete fulfillment," she responded.

"How do you come to see these things as evils?" I asked.

"I didn't use the word evil, you did. Certainly there are few things more gratifying to human beings than work. It is one way to feel purposeful and fulfilled. Work provides a stimulating avenue for actualizing yourself. But working for money, or even for what it can buy, is another dead-end proposition. On Earth you cannot reach personal fulfillment through external means because happiness is an internal process. If you are happy, it is because you experience it within."

"But doesn't having money provide you with a better avenue for achieving inner happiness?" I asked.

"Not at all. This is one of those mistaken assumptions that business-minded people would love to have everyone else believe. The idea that having money leads to happiness just isn't so. If you could only see your world as I do, through *reality-only* lenses, you would have a different point of view. There are some four billion people on your planet. Less than 1 or 2 percent of all those people have abundant supplies of money. Thus 98 percent of your people lack money, and yet the poorest among them are capable of being happy, of enjoying a sunset, a family get-together, or anything at all. Conversely, the richest among you are capable of the highest depression and suicide rates, of feeling empty inside even with full bellies and all of life's embellishments. While you would like everyone to believe that money makes for happiness, I'm sorry to disappoint you. It has nothing to do with what genuine happiness is."

"If money has nothing to do with happiness, then why do people pursue it so vigorously?" I responded.

"Because their thinking is wrong. They've convinced themselves that security and happiness will result from accumulating purchasing power. Or they believe that they must accumulate money in order to be a responsible person. They sacrifice. They do things they dislike, such as staying in a routine job, or living in a city they dislike, in the name of responsibility or the pursuit of happiness. Money has nothing to do with either one.''

"Please go on," I implored. "I don't see how people on Earth can really be responsible if they don't try to better themselves and work for the money that will bring about a higher quality of life.''

"You are slavishly holding on to the 'money is happiness and responsibility' doctrine that permeates so many of your cultures. All this fear about being irresponsible and not meeting your obligations to your loved ones is a myth. It's only a product of looking at your world and fearing what *might* happen. In reality, the problems are only inventions of the mind. If you meet a person who has always been responsible, who has met all obligations to family and to self, then that is his or her reality and ought to be the basis of that person's thinking. But instead people believe that success came from the job, the money, the luck, the lack of a recession, or something else that's external. Consequently they start thinking incorrectly and inventing catastrophes that are not rooted in reality. Because people on Earth are loath to accept credit for their own success, they look outside of themselves, both for credit and for blame.

"If you had workers looking inside and taking responsibility for themselves, they would know that they could go anywhere on your planet and be successful. Their success would not be related to external events, economic conditions, or luck. Instead, it would be an inner process which could never be taken away." After pausing for a drink of water, she continued, "Besides, your people don't understand the real irony of working for money."

"And just what is that irony?" I asked in my most businesslike manner.

"If you pursue your own ideals and enjoy what you do because that is how you choose to think, success will come to you in ways and abundance beyond your dreams," she stated.

"But surely you don't believe that money will simply come to you?" I asked incredulously.

"Success will arrive in your life in whatever form you need it. All your creative geniuses—your artists, musicians, architects, statesmen, writers, actors, businessmen, chefs, designers, mechanics—do not do what they do for money, even though it may appear that way to you. Can you imagine a master artist saying to himself, 'This one will bring in so many dollars'? Not at all! The actual act of doing whatever it is that you do should provide satisfaction to you independently of any external reward. Even your best-paid athletes do not perform for the money itself. Do you think a ball player who is paid less one season works harder in the actual performance of his duties the next year, when he's paid more? The payment is a bonus. The bonuses arrive when you stop focusing on them and turn your thoughts to enjoying your life and what you're doing," she concluded.

"So you think that we place far too much emphasis on accumulations and appearances rather than on the quality of the experiences themselves," I said, trying to summarize and remembering what she had said to me at our last meeting.

"I think you believe that the accumulations and appearances have the potential for happiness within them, and this is wrong," she said, correcting my conclusions.

"But if accumulating money for buying things to make one happy is wrong, why do so many people do it?" I asked again.

"Because here you perpetuate so well the myth of happiness as an external process. There's nothing wrong with the words 'profit' or 'money.' I heartily endorse them for what they are. I just see Earthlings confusing these concepts with personal happiness and fulfillment," she responded.

"Well then, what are the purposes of money and profits on Earth, as you see them?"

"They serve as a medium of exchange, a way to transfer goods and services between people of all backgrounds and skills, and this is a wonderful thing. This is the reality purpose," she said.

"Would you encourage people to work to improve the quality of their lives by raising their incomes and searching for promotions?" I asked.

"The quality of life on Earth is related to money only in your mind, not in reality. I repeat, not in reality. I saw people living on remote islands who had not one coin to their names, baking their own bread. They were happy, contented human beings who wanted no more. I saw executives in the most posh homes with uncountable collections of coins who were unhappy to the point of severe depression. Their children were suicidal with fear that they didn't have the skills to hang on to the amassed wealth. I would encourage people to work for the joy of what they are doing, to take pride and fulfillment in their acts, whatever they may be, and just for the acts themselves. If they can't do that, I would encourage them to look for other activities that they find fulfilling. I would encourage management to focus on what they can do to make all work personally fulfilling. The people of your world must try to find joy and serenity within themselves and take that energy into everything they do. If they follow this path, the symbols of success will follow, and will arrive in sufficient amounts. People who continue to chase the symbols of success will find these symbols always eluding them, and, even more devastatingly, they will suffer from the widespread disease of MORE." She stopped and looked right at me. "Have I said it clearly enough?" she asked.

"Quite," I replied, "but what is the disease of more?"

"On Earth, *more* is the sickness that keeps people from ever arriving at *now*. You have a world of strivers when you could have a world of arrivers. When you work for money and what it can bring you in the future, then 'what-it-can-bring-in-the-future' becomes the reason for working and accumulating money. This means that no matter how much you accumulate, you'll never arrive, because what you have can only be seen for 'what-it-will-bring-in-the-future.' I've seen business people seriously afflicted with this 'more' malady. They have accumulated more than they could ever spend, and yet they use their minds to remind themselves that they must still acquire more. They pursue 'more' and 'better' to such an extent that they destroy themselves and begin to believe in an even more destructive form of wrong thinking. They subscribe to the incorrect thought that *they are what they do*," she said.

"And why is this so destructive?" I asked.

"Because it is simply wrong again. Once you believe your values derive from what you accomplish, then it must also follow that when you fail to accomplish, then you have no value. Hence you see people all over your planet who, when their 'profit pictures' turn sour, become depressed, even to the point of needing treatment from others who are suffering from 'more.' I've observed humans feeling useless when they retire because they believe they are what they do. I've seen people afraid of failing when it is clear that on Earth you can't grow unless you are willing to fail—a lot! The truth as I see it is that your value as a person comes from what you decide to believe about yourself, not from any accumulations or accomplishments. And when you confuse this, you set yourself up for pain, regardless of how well you defend your beliefs. Does this make sense to you?"

"Yes, but what are the most common manifestations of the pain? After all, not everyone in the business world is on the verge of suicide or even mildly depressed," I shot right back.

"The symptoms I've observed are reflected in almost all walks of life for those so afflicted, and it all stems from the incorrect thinking I've mentioned so many times. For example, I heard many businessmen saying that the most important things in their lives were their loved ones, their families, and the assurance that these people would be happy. Yet these businessmen spent almost no time with their loved ones. They were busy accumulating money, which they must have believed would provide that happiness. Still, their marriages were breaking up and they were clearly strangers to their own children. Ironically, they had no time to be with the very people they described as most important to them.

"You see, their thinking is in error. They know within themselves that they can't buy happiness, and still they spend their days attempting to do just that. In addition, they are often infected with 'hurry sickness.' They are almost always rushing, even when they have no reality-based reason for doing so. They become obsessed with perfection, using in their personal lives the same *assets-versus-liabilities* approach that works so well in their businesses. I often saw them making unrealistic demands on their families, insisting that they behave like statistics on a ledger, and then wondering why the families became lost to them. Moreover, their own bodies were often racked with ulcers, high blood pressure, borderline alcoholism, and anxiety. These are the payoffs for locating happiness outside yourself, and pursuing the false symbols of success, of which the dollar sign is the most prominent. This money lust seems to run rampant, almost unchecked, on Earth, and all for nothing. People just think incorrectly and raise their offspring to do precisely the same."

"But it isn't all bad. Don't you think that industrialization has raised the standard of living around the world?" I protested.

"I didn't say that working and money were bad. If you recall, I said that the way it's perceived and utilized in your world is the problem. I support working as a high-level way to live your life and feel worthy at the same time. But your question also presupposes a truth that simply does not exist in your reality—that the industrialized world is better than the nonindustrialized world. If you look at it realistically, for every higher standard of living of which you boast, there are expensive prices to pay. If you improve transportation, you pollute the air. If you build great factories you fill your world with carcinogens. If you build great weapons you prepare to destroy your world in a conflagration that is too evil to contemplate.

"In those 'uncivilized' places where living standards are so low, people don't carry guns or die of cancer. While they can't move about as freely as others, they don't breathe and drink industrial waste. They live on their land rather than storing nuclear weapons on it. They're close to their loved ones and don't need to drink liquor to get through their day. In reality, a higher standard of living is a businessman's justification for almost everything he does, and yet when he is most honest with himself, he will say, 'We were happiest in the days when we had very little. We genuinely loved each other when our goals were only dreams. Sharing them brought us closer together. The lean years offered so little in the way of externals that we had to turn inward.' And that is the nature of happiness. You see, all your suffering comes from craving and desire. When you stop to simply live and enjoy, suffering also diminishes. Don't be too quick to jump to the conclusion that those 'uncivilized' folks with lower living standards have a corner on misery and an absence of fulfillment and happiness. In fact, you have much to learn from each other. Instead of defending your great monetary profit system, which needs no defense, since it works well, look to what you are doing with it, what you believe it holds for you in the way of happiness. If you can't be just as happy working in your garden as you are in a fancy night club or working out a business deal, then you've yet to understand that basic truth of your Earthly reality. That is, as I said before, *there is no way to happiness, happiness is the way.*"

We had completed two intense discussions and Eykis was as relaxed now as she had been an hour earlier. It was no effort for her to be honest. She was just as at home talking about religion or management as a kid at a picnic. She was natural, expressive, and willing to sample anything that was offered. There was no need for her to try to impress with her vocabulary or cite statistical evidence for her assertions. She didn't have to quote scholars to buttress her viewpoints. She was her own kind of expert.

I moved to the next subject, introducing myself as a leading educator. I asked her about educational practices on Uranus, and what she had observed of educational attitudes and institutions on Earth.

"How do you view our educational practices, Eykis?" I asked, making it as open-ended a beginning as possible.

"The most alarming thing to me about your entire formal educational system is the huge gap between what you say you're doing and what is actually being done. In virtually all your administrative statements about education, you declare that your purpose is to encourage individual thinking, self-actualization, an opportunity for each child to maximize his potential as a free-thinking person. But I've not seen any practices that carry out these lofty objectives,'' she said.

"Where do you see evidence of this gap?"

"In almost all your schools. Every time young people seem to be displaying any creative or free-thinking qualities, they are perceived as threats and instantly squelched. Few teachers can stand a child who asks, 'Why?' Your educational rewards are doled out to those who conform the best, to those who please their teachers or do their assignments quickly and neatly. There are few rewards for independent thinking; in fact in most instances it appears to be punished. A child who is truly independent of the need for approval, who shows no signs of guilt or anxiety about it, is considered a troublemaker. A child who refuses to be just like everybody else is singled out and asked to feel guilty and repent. Yet these qualities of being guilt-free, independent, and free thinking are what you label as no-limit or self-actualized behaviors. Again, it just seems unreal to me to find you stating one thing as an educational objective and doing exactly the opposite.''

"But children need to be disciplined first so that they can later make free, independent judgments. That's why we stress doing it right, or the 'teacher's way.' Besides, if everyone did whatever he wanted, there would be no discipline and it would be literally impossible to teach a class," I stated in my best "educationese."

"I find it impossible to imagine how a child can learn to be a free thinker by being trained for the opposite. It would be like training someone to be a great runner by forcing him to sit down all his life. A classroom in which children are all busily pursuing individual objectives isn't necessarily a chaotic one. It could be one in which there's excitement, instead of the apathy I noted in virtually every classroom on your planet. Individuals could be helping each other in classrooms. They could have busy, creative arenas, a miniature real world if you will, for exploring any subject at all. Instead, students are told to sit in their assigned seats and quietly do as they're told. This leads straight to the incorrect, neurotic thinking we have discussed."

"Do you feel that an entire classroom sitting quietly is not a proper learning environment?"

"It's not a question of proper or improper environment. It simply is not a learning environment. You know each person in your world is unique and special. How can you tap that uniqueness when each child is treated the same way?" she asked me.

"But I don't see how that is being done in our classrooms on Earth," I protested.

"Well, here's what I observed. On Monday a teacher introduces a new subject, Egyptian history, say. The teacher gives the same material to every student. They are all exposed to the same lecture and discussion, they all read the same book, they all do the same homework assignments, and on Friday they are all given the same tests. Do you follow and agree so far?'' she asked.

''Yes, yes, go on,'' I said.

''The students who perform best on the test are given an A, those who 'pass' receive a C or a D, and some fail. There are no provisions for those individual differences that are an integral part of your reality. Why is it assumed that everyone will assimilate such information at the same rate? Why is the student who got only half the answers correct because he may need two weeks to learn the material punished with a low grade? Why should they all be expected to perform at exactly the same rate? What about the students who need only a day to master Egyptian history but need fifteen days for long division? Why are they forced to sit there quietly listening to material they've already mastered? I'll tell you why if you're interested.''

''Please do,'' I said.

''The answer is, you treat them all the same. You teach them all the same way, in the same amount of time, and call those who can learn exactly that way the fastest, the smartest. In my reality, being able to assimilate something faster than someone else has to do with one thing, speed. Your educational logic guarantees there will always be average and below average students. You insist that everyone conform to a standard norm. You teach all your young people to think and act alike. But what do you have to offer your world if you are just like everybody else? You insure this through the insane pursuit of grades, those educational merit badges you dispense on report cards and transcripts. These are the real obsession of educators on Earth—not knowledge and self-discovery, but the pursuit of those external rewards called grades. Moreover, these grades that you've elevated to this almighty status have absolutely nothing to do with being educated in reality," she declared hotly. This seemed to be an area that Urantians felt very strongly about.

"But what's wrong with providing rewards in the form of grades for educational excellence?" I asked.

"Grades and knowledge are mutually exclusive ideas. In fact, grades actually serve to lower motivation for knowledge," she replied.

"Why are they mutually exclusive?" I asked.

"A grade is an external mark. It signifies for an individual that he/she has participated in the game of education. Knowledge is an inner mark. It is reflected in (1) how you feel about what you've learned, (2) how it aids you in pursuing your ideals, and (3) what you as a person can do with that knowledge. Knowledge breeds self-awareness: grades breed self-deception. A grade on a transcript has nothing to do with reality. It is a symbol of having conformed, and even here on Earth, where people misperceive their reality so regularly, grades still have very little relation to reality. Nobody looks at a transcript two years after college, and certainly you wouldn't want to assess a grownup person's ability on the basis of an academic transcript. The person who received all As only a year ago might fail every one of those same examinations today. On Earth, it's how well you currently produce that earns you respect and personal advancement.

"Oftentimes those who can play the academic game

well are actually ill equipped to participate in the real world. And on the other hand, many who refuse to pursue grades neurotically in school turn out to be more reality oriented and hence much more successful at virtually everything they do. Plain and simple, the educational world on Earth seems to be located in an 'unreal' sphere,'' she said.

"But you said earlier that grades actually lower motivation in individuals. Do you mean to tell me that you think our educational system actually detracts from human motivation on Earth?" I asked.

"Precisely," she said. "When you place an Earth person in a system in which the reward—the grade— is unrelated to the actual learning activity, motivation is lowered. For example, if you give an A to a person who reads five books, or completes fifty push-ups, a B for four books and forty push-ups, and so on down the line, who do you think will ever want to read a hundred books or do a thousand push-ups? Almost no one, that's who. Your system says, strive for the reward and work only when you are being rewarded. Since the reward of an A has nothing to do in reality with either reading or push-ups, then motivation will cease when the reward is achieved," she concluded.

"So how could it be changed?" I asked.

"First, the rewards for learning must be aligned with the actual activity of learning. The reward for reading is not located on a transcript, it's within. It's the joy of being able to comprehend life through writers, the thrill of getting lost in a novel or discovering and applying a new idea; the freedom one achieves by being able to experience what others have thought;

the inner glow and self-satisfaction of reading for personal growth. These are the rewards of reading. Similarly, the personal sense of accomplishment one feels when he is in top physical condition, the glorious feeling that comes from being physically fit, the ability to climb stairs without pausing to catch your breath, to run without feeling exhausted, to eat and sleep peacefully, to bask in your own self-pride at being superbly healthy—these are the rewards for doing push-ups. When you begin to align your rewards in education with the actual educational activity, motivation will increase and apathy will decline, and not one moment before,'' she said emphatically.

"And teachers, what about their role?" I asked.

"When it comes to teachers you again confuse your reality. On Earth, no one can teach you anything. You make a decision to know what you know, and any experienced teacher will tell you that when confronted with a student who has decided not to know something, such as algebra, no amount of 'teaching' is going to get that algebra across. That is your reality. Conversely, when a student decides to learn algebra, no amount of teacher interference will alter that decision. It seems to me that all Earthlings have the inner capacity to learn anything either with the aid of, or in spite of, teachers. Truly great teachers understand this, and deliberately go about their business of providing a unique environment for individuals to make choices to learn. Furthermore, they emphasize learning for mastery, rather than striving for grades."

"What do you mean by learning for mastery?"

"Mastery means that the goal of education is to

master the curriculum. How long it takes is quite irrelevant. It means that individuals take tests when
they are ready to see how much they have mastered,
rather than on a test day set aside for everyone. Mastery means no punishment for being slower or faster
at mastering a subject. Mastery means that when you
acquire knowledge, you get inner satisfaction, plus the
A if you need the grade for record-keeping purposes.
The results are personal satisfaction and inner pride,
and one receives a grade of *Mastery* when he demon-
strates mastery of the material. In a mastery system,
people want to help each other, rather than compete
for the few trophies that educators make available in
the form of grades, honor societies, and the like. Students have freedom to develop in areas of personal
interest and explore challenging subjects without fear
of 'failing.' Cooperation rather than competition is the
style of learning, and cheating is impossible," she
said.

"Cheating is impossible?" I repeated.

"Yes, how could anyone cheat when the goal of
education is to assist each individual toward his own
levels of excellence? Tell me, how can you cheat when
the rewards are inner rather than outer-directed?"

"Well, I never thought about it like that," I said.

"Imagine a person taking a test to see how prepared
he or she is to move on to the next level of learning.
That person is going to assess his or her own progress
on any given subject. How could anybody cheat? I
saw a study in which you Earthlings tested chickens
to see which ones were dumb and which smart. A
length of chicken wire was set up in front of their feed,

and the ones you labeled dumb sat still and ultimately died of starvation. The chickens you labeled smart walked around the barrier and got at their food. Now when chickens go around barriers for their external rewards, they're labeled smart, but when students do the same thing, you label it cheating.''

''But how could we possibly allow children to copy from each other without punishing them! Don't they have to learn self-reliance, which you seem to feel is lacking?'' I asked.

''Children can be encouraged to help each other achieve their maximum personal knowledge levels. In a world of individuals, comparing children to each other is a senseless activity. If your children were in an educational system that prized knowledge, they would soon learn cooperation rather than competition. Your entire world is composed of people competing against each other. While competition without scorn on a playground is fun and healthy, in the real world it breeds antagonisms, hatreds, nationalism, and theories of racial superiority. The schools are the one place where you can begin to foster a sense of working together. What would a child have to gain by copying for an examination in a mastery arrangement? absolutely nothing! The purpose of the exam is not to reward or to punish, but to help young people assess their personal progress. There shouldn't be any stultifying group examinations or comparison of results. These would be replaced by a healthy atmosphere of cooperation and helping. If this same quality were transferred to your governments, you would end most of the petty squabbles and power plays that create wars and bitter hatreds. Teachers can do a great deal toward basing education on knowledge rather than the competitive acquisitions mentality that currently exists."

"How?" I asked. I wanted her to be specific.

"They can get the external-reward, money-oriented business philosophy out of education. Students confronted with a rigid, authoritarian teacher will perform only in the presence of that authoritarian figure. As is true in business, when the authoritarian teacher leaves the room, students abandon the pretense. If those authoritarian teachers, who take so much pride in their well-disciplined classrooms, could only look at their classrooms when they are not there, they would soon see the results of their rigidity. The fact is that when formal schooling is complete, the teachers are permanently out of the room. Students who have been exposed to them for long periods of time dally for the rest of their lives. They soon despise all learning activities because they are associated with rigid authoritarian thinking. Teachers in a reality-only system of mastery learning are educating young people to become their own teachers. The presence of the authority figure in the room has nothing to do with the individual pursuit of knowledge and excellence. I've noticed here that in colleges and institutions of higher education the students actually buy their knowledge points with money. Those who stay with it and purchase more credits receive the highest external educational rewards. Yet your world is populated with Ph.D.s and many others who have purchased considerable knowledge credits and can't even write a clear thought, much less get a job. The only jobs they seem to want are those that provide them with institutional credibility for helping others purchase more external knowledge points.''

''Do you have any final thoughts on how we can make our educational systems more effective?'' I asked, indicating that we were drawing to a close on this subject.

''It's simply a matter of becoming more reality based. Knowledge is internal. Acquisitions are external. You say you're concerned about knowledge and the inner person, yet all your educational energy is channeled to externals such as grades, test scores, diplomas, degrees, and titles. Educating for knowledge, which your reality permits so nicely, is missing because your educators are thinking incorrectly about *ends*, as opposed to putting your energy into *means* which reflect a world of unique individuals all of whom deserve specialized education. Your children can emerge from their educational experiences excited about the prospects of being knowledgeable for the pure joy it brings, as well as the limitless opportunities available to a person of knowledge. But too often they emerge from the educational maze like one of the flock, looking, thinking, and bleating just like everyone else,'' she said, and stopped right there.

I never grew weary talking with Eykis. She had deliberately minimized references to Uranus during our three conversations because her gifts were not to be a comparison of our two worlds but a legacy for all of us on Earth from someone who viewed us through special eyes. She had conveyed to me what Uranus was like. She had been surprised at the "unreal," or. as she called it, "incorrect" thinking she had found in her initial observations of us. Like any realist she had internalized what she noted and accepted us as we are. Yet she knew how to slice through what "we are" when it masked what we "could become." As she had said to me several times, "On Uranus we are trapped by our reality, but your potential for magnificence as a whole plane of free thinkers is almost unimaginable." It was in this context that she offered her gifts. She didn't want to create a wordy document. Instead, she was giving us wonderfully honest and sensible briefings, and I was content now to become another character for Eykis to inform in her own peerless style.

"I represent the practice of medicine," I said. "What have you noticed about my profession in your visit here?"

"I'm really quite surprised at your planet's perceptions of health. A philosophy of sickness rather than wellness seems to run through the general population as well as the medical community," she said.

"What do you mean by sickness philosophy?" I asked her.

"I am accustomed to a very different approach to medicine. On Uranus the patient pays his doctor a monthly retainer to keep him healthy. If he becomes ill, payments stop until the doctor gets him well. On Earth, people expect to get sick. They program themselves to anticipate getting worse. Those who think 'sick' come to believe they can't get healthy again without medical treatment and drugs. This, once again, is incorrect thinking, and it manifests itself particularly in the way you view your bodies and in your expectations for being healthy.

"Your health is directly related to how you use your minds. Those of you who think positively about yourselves have positive expectations all through life. This includes your expectations for wellness. I've noticed people saying things like 'I feel a cold coming on. It will probably get worse and be in my chest tomorrow. I expect I'll have a fever soon and have to take a few days off from work this week.' And sure enough, these people create a self-fulfilling sickness prophecy. I've further noticed that when people expect to get worse, they seldom disappoint themselves," she said.

"So you feel that if people were taught to think differently, that is *correctly,* as you put it, that they wouldn't be afflicted with colds and other minor ailments?" I asked.

"Precisely. I've seen positive thinking represented on Earth. Those people who don't focus on their ailments, who actually expect a minor cold or flu symptom to improve rather than get worse, who don't complain to others, are much less susceptible to these maladies. You are lucky here on Earth. Health is, for the most part, a choice. You can choose to be healthy, but few of you do it," she added.

"But what do you mean by *choice?*" I asked. "Surely you don't think people choose all their illnesses?"

"Yes, I do, with inherited debilities being the only exceptions, and even the extent to which these 'unchosen afflictions' immobilize a patient is directly related to attitudes and choices. Look, let me turn it around and ask you, the doctor, a question. Is there anything you would trade for your good health?"

"Nothing. Without good health one would die," I responded.

"So you see, it is the single most important facet of your personal life, correct?" she asked.

"Certainly. Nothing is more important to an individual than good health. I think everyone here would agree with that, since ultimately an absence of health means an end to life," I answered.

"Then would you please explain to me why so few of you think and behave in ways that are healthy if health is at the top of your list of personal priorities? This kind of unhealthy thinking is really a mystery to me."

"I'm not sure I know what you mean by unhealthy thinking," I said.

"Attitudes toward sickness and health," she snapped back. "You consume things that anyone can see are poison in countless quantities. Tobacco, alcohol, fatty foods, preservatives, drugs—you seem to treat your bodies as if you didn't know that these self-defeating attitudes which lead to self-destructive behaviors are harmful. Yet you know they are. You print warnings on your packages, and people still consume these poisons. It's all a choice," she said.

"Do you think this is another reflection of our wrong thinking?" I asked.

"Of course it is. You've trained yourselves to think in sick ways, and you've also trained yourselves to fulfill this sickness thinking in the ways you live. But

it goes far beyond poor body habits and thinking sick.
It has to do with how you approach this whole business of holistic versus sickness thinking. Your medical
profession is sickness rather than wellness oriented.
Everyone teaches about illness. Almost no one
teaches about health. Your doctors see patients when
they don't feel well, or when something overtly appears to be wrong. Their role is to correct what has
gone wrong, or, more precisely, what has been allowed to go wrong. People on Earth go to doctors to
be fixed up and brought back to normal. No one seems
to think about living beyond the normal, especially
those in the medical and helping professions,'' she
said.

"We doctors do have to operate this way, we have
to treat those in need,'' I offered, still assuming the
role of a leading medical practitioner.

"Why not a medical profession which helps people
to transcend their sickness thinking and uses doctors
primarily as persons who help people to become as
healthy as possible, and only secondarily as repairers
of the sick?'' Eykis asked.

"We do try to teach preventive medicine and holistic thinking. We are simply overworked and over-
crowded, with so many sick people that current work
loads preclude shifting gears to what you propose,'' I
stated.

"That too is incorrect thinking. The medical world
relies on its sickness mentality and reinforces it in
virtually all of its practices. Doctors are the ones dispensing those huge numbers of tranquilizers used for
your nonexistent anxiety attacks. It is doctors who

perform the unnecessary surgery that has become a way of life in medical practices. Doctors hurriedly write out prescriptions for every ailment on your planet, largely because they are victims of their own erroneous thinking.''

"How are we victims of our thinking?" I asked somewhat testily.

"You think that you are the healers, and that the medicines you dispense are doing the healing within the body. This is incorrect," she stated firmly.

"But how can you say that? Look at what medicine has done on our planet. Life expectancies have increased, some forms of virulent diseases have been eradicated, and doctors improve people's lives every day," I reminded her.

"Of course, many diseases have been eliminated and life expectancies have increased, but let's give the credit where it belongs. The body, not you, is the hero! Your bodies are perfect creations. No doctor can heal a broken bone. Only a body which is working properly can do that. No doctor can eliminate polio; only bodies can do that, by building up inner resistances. Just because you administer the immunization and write out the prescription doesn't mean that you are the healer. As educators must train their young to be their own teachers, and parents must aid their children to become their own parents, so, too, must doctors teach their patients to become their own doctors. Each person must be taught to use his own inherent healing properties. But most doctors don't do this because they don't believe in it. They choose to believe that they actually do the healing. Consequently they perpetuate the very same incorrect thinking which leads to so much unnecessary sickness in your world.''

"It sounds as if you have very little regard for our medical profession,'' I said.

"Quite the contrary,'' Eykis shot right back. "The medical profession is perhaps the most advanced of all of your institutions. The training methods for weeding out incompetence are superb. The people are highly motivated and actually exceedingly competent. What needs repair are the incorrect beliefs about what constitutes health services, and who does the healing,'' she said.

"And how would you help to correct this?'' I asked.

"First, I would help the medical profession to see the advantages of holistic wellness thinking. I could envision people going to their doctors, not because they were sick, but because they wanted to get even healthier. Doctors could serve primarily to help people acquire mental attitudes which would preclude psychosomatic illnesses. They could monitor their nutrition intake, their exercise, their heart rate, their lung power, blood count, and endurance. People would begin seeing doctors not as rectifiers to achieve normalcy, but as people who helped them go beyond basic normal health to super health. People would become wellness oriented. Doctors would facilitate this from birth, instead of fighting it and acting as if anyone who comes along and recommends anything other than drugs or surgery is a quack. Doctors seem to fear innovation, despite their involvement in research, particularly as it relates to human health. In Western cultures they are usually the first to reject any nondrug or nonmedical approach to human health. Such practices as meditation, biofeedback, hypnosis, yoga, nutritional therapy, acupuncture, or anything else which they know little about, are immediately denounced as shams by the medical profession, and it often takes many years for doctors to accept them even grudgingly. You seem to be exceedingly protective of your one-way approach to health and extremely reluctant to admit that there may be other approaches that could be combined with traditional medical practices to create an entire network of wellness-oriented practitioners.''

"And then?'' I said, wanting her to go on.

"And then I would reexamine the proclivity you have for hanging onto medicines as healers. You must look toward the vast mending potential of your minds. I would train people to stop seeking external miracle cures and begin looking inward, to examine the limitless capacity that your mind and body have for convalescence and health. So much of your Earthly sickness is located in your minds. This is due to a lifetime of expectation that some sickness is normal, and that when it comes along it should be treated with external rather than internal elixirs. Moreover, I would look at your medical beliefs themselves, such as the routine use of surgery to remove healthy organs in the body, and immobilization for virtually all ailments, when perhaps vigorous exercise to promote circulation would be more conducive to health. So much of your medical thinking seems to center on the notion that people are weak and fragile, and that an injury always requires rest. Yet the time it takes for healing is greatly decreased in active people. Activity is almost always frowned upon, largely because so many doctors appear to be a much more sedentary lot than I had imagined they would be.

"I see doctors smoking and drinking, often overweight, and actually becoming addicted themselves, while simultaneously dispensing medical advice. This is a prospect that I must confess eludes my logical mind. I see the overemphasis on drugs as a major area of medical malpractice. Drugs for headaches, cramps, tension, and even anxiety. This overreliance on drugs comes from your external mindset in medicine. You believe that something outside the person caused the illness (such as a virus going around, the cold season, flu bugs, old age, a draft), and consequently you look to something outside yourselves for a cure. This attitude explains your overreliance on drugs and your obsession with tablets as panaceas for everything. But the process of healing, like everything else, is already located within those patients you treat. Positive attitudes toward health as a means of abolishing sickness, and the mind as healer, are often treated as heresy by doctors, who cannot see the truth because they are blinded by their own rigid education."

"And that truth is?" I inserted.

"And that truth is that no doctor on your planet has ever healed anyone. The mind and body do the healing, and doctor's treatments can only facilitate that process. Until doctors educate themselves and their patients on the great healing capacities of your perfect bodies, you will continue to have a world which is becoming increasingly and needlessly drug dependent," she concluded.

"Can people really alter their proclivity toward serious illness with their minds?" I asked.

"Positively. Your mind is the captain of the ship called your body. Whatever is going on inside it, is controlled by that captain, and he uses only a tiny fragment of his potential in the process of being well. Every doctor on your planet knows about the *will to live*. They can't directly put their fingers on it, but they know that patients with a strong will to live have a much greater chance of surviving any serious illness or major surgery. That *will* needs to be cultivated in everyone and reflected in healthful, wellness-oriented approaches toward life.

"Doctors seldom question the ability of the mind to be destructive. They know that a 'tense thinking' mind can actually create an ulcer or high blood pressure. But somehow they find it difficult to act as if they believe that that same mind is capable of curing the ulcer, or lowering the blood pressure. Instead they rely on drugs. They know that the mind can alter the chemistry of the body and promote disease, yet they disdain those who train the same mind to reverse the process. The medical profession still wants to hang onto medicine and treatment as the approach to health, largely because doctors practice external incorrect thinking. When you begin to see the limitless potential of the human body for healing itself, you will be taking a big step forward. Then you can prescribe your medicines as ancillary to the healing process, and put the focus of healing where it belongs, within the patient. As always the inner person is ignored by professionals of all stripes, and your medical profession is no exception. You have an advantage over us on Uranus in that your *within* is controlled by free will, yet you seldom take advantage of it for your own benefit.''

She could have gone on telling me about our medical practices, but we had a great deal left to discuss, and the day was going by much too quickly.

''I would like very much to know your reaction to our governments and how they serve our people here on Earth,'' I said to Eykis, shifting to my fifth and final role of the morning.

''Your governments do not serve your people. They are not designed for such purposes,'' she answered without a change of expression.

''What are their purposes then, as you see them, Eykis?''

''They are created to serve the ends of those who work in them, although they all say that they are created to serve the will of the people.''

''Do you think all governments ignore the will of the people?'' I asked her.

''Yes, although some do it to a much greater degree than others. Governments here seem to be in the power business. When those who are outside your governments try to gain control of the reins of power, they talk about how the will of the people is being subverted, and then, when they manage to get into the government, they proceed to behave the same way themselves. Somehow, on Earth, power itself seems to corrupt, and those who are in power are much more interested in expanding their spheres of influence than in actually serving the needs and wishes of the people," she said.

"As a representative of governments, I'd like you to explain to me how you see this taking place," I said in my best semidemanding tone, befitting a government official in a position of world leadership.

"Fine," she said. "I'll be happy to. If you take a poll of all the peoples on Earth, you will find that with the exception of a small group of your generals and a handful of soldiers, every single person on your planet wants peace—not war. Yet you are constantly at war with each other. Moreover, your entire planet stands precariously at the edge of total extinction through the stockpiling of unwanted nuclear weapons. People on Earth want to live harmoniously. I know, I looked into this all over your world. Yet your governments still act in ways that contradict the people's wishes. All your wars have been brought about by government people who decide to send your young men and women off to die. These young people obey commands, such as killing fellow humans, that conflict deeply with what they feel as humans, yet they do it. You all want peace, yet your governments keep all the people of your planet either at war or on the brink of war."

"But war and readiness for war are necessary reactions to avoid being conquered by enemies. And like it or not, that is our reality," I said.

"If you devoted the same energy and money to peace and to helping people use their individuality, you would eliminate war. You fail to see that killing each other is the absolute lowest level to which humans can sink. Yet your people do everything possible to keep your society on a level that always blames the *enemy* for your own lowest level of thinking," she said.

"But how can the training to be individuals do anything but create anarchy and increase the possibility of war?" I asked.

"You must begin to use your vast government powers to train individuals to think ethically. A world of ethical thinkers would not create warriors. Ethical people would refuse to invent something as evil as napalm. No salesman could ever sell it. No factory personnel could ever mass produce it. No trucker could ever transport it. No generals could ever order it to be used on people. And no soldiers could ever scorch human bodies with it. You see, the entire chain of human beings that creates something as devastatingly stupid and evil as war is broken when you have individuals who think ethically, rather than like the herd. One individual, deciding to trust his inner voices, can break a chain that depends on blind obedience for its very survival. Once you begin to use your governments for such a purpose, you will defeat the ugliness of war forever. Make no mistake about it, the governments of the world have the power to make this happen."

"But can we tolerate too many of these free-willed, ethical individuals if we are to survive?" I asked.

"Your survival as a people depends solely on individual thinkers. Look at the most repressive of all of your governments. The totalitarian and dictatorial regimes that populate your planet are most successful where people think like the herd, not as individuals. These people are trained in conformity and nationalism, racial pride and historical animosities. They all think alike. They are obedient because they are told to be that way. Conversely, your freest societies were built on individualism. They were founded by people leaving repressive governments, religious fascism, and the divine right of kings. Throughout your history authoritarianism has failed to take hold where people were encouraged to think for themselves and to question absolute authority. Great societies are composed of great individuals who refuse to be told how to think and act as a unit. Totalitarianism and dictatorships flourish only when large collections of people suspend their individuality for the betterment of the state. The proof of your Earthly capacity for individualism can be seen by those who risk death to speak out while living in dictatorial nations. Individual freedom of thought is a flame not easily extinguished," she said.

"But you said earlier that *all* of our governments fail to serve the will of the people," I reminded her.

"You're right, and I said it because it's so. The degree to which the people's will is submerged is greater in places where individuals are not permitted to express their own unique thoughts when they conflict with the official views of the government, but the will of the people is seldom the primary consideration of any government. The individuals who comprise the government are more concerned with themselves than those they are pledged to serve. For example, your government passes laws requiring mandatory retirement ages in various occupations and votes to exempt members of the government from the *benefit* of these very same laws. They vote to allow themselves special treatment in declaring expenses, and deny these same privileges to everyone in the country except lawmakers. They vote social security taxes which are almost confiscatory and exempt themselves from having to pay. They pass civil rights laws and exempt themselves from the provisions of the law that apply to all but the privileged lawmakers. They tell the people to sacrifice and yet the people are expected to pay for limousines and drivers for government representatives who use the money of the people to pay for their special privileges. They refuse to legislate medical benefits for the people, and then use the people's money to create their own medical insurance, which, incidentally, involves the most comprehensive free medical attention available anywhere on this planet. The fact is that the government representatives on Earth, be they elected or self-appointed, serve themselves, with the earnings of the people," she said, her voice almost racing by now.

"But isn't government necessary, even if it corrupts its representatives?" I asked.

"Do not be mistaken about this. Governments do NOT corrupt their representatives, the representatives corrupt their governments," she stated emphatically. "Of course government is necessary, but you must look carefully at what you expect from the people in your government. If you want them to think and act for you, the results will be the kind of unresponsive governments that you've created. You seem to forget that power is only in the hands of the government because your people allow it. With so many externally oriented 'wrong thinkers' in your world, it is not surprising that your governments take on the same flavor. You want your governments to do everything for you, and then you complain because they take away your freedom. You can't have it both ways."

"So what can we do to make governments responsive to the will of the people?" I asked.

"Take responsibility for your own lives rather than asking the government to do it for you," she declared, adding: "The real function of government is not to control the people, but to provide the people with a means for creating a society that works. Yet your governments seem preoccupied with controlling, monitoring, regulating, and snooping into everyone's daily life. You regulate literally every aspect of human enterprise on your planet. You have government rules, forms, red tape, and regulatory procedures for everything from transportation to sexual conduct. You have rules on every subject that affect every one of you, and you give the government the responsibility for making your societies work. For example, your governments debate the issue of abortion endlessly and pass laws about it, never for a moment understanding that the very existence of those laws creates horrible conditions. A woman who wants an abortion, for whatever reason, isn't going to be deterred because it is illegal. Legality is unrelated to her decision. She will abort if she chooses, but if there is a law against it, the existence of that law will increase her likelihood of unprofessional medical care and possibly her own death. Government people pass unethical laws all the time, but those laws are not what determine people's behavior at all."

"But people are basically law abiding," I said.

"When the laws make sense. And when they don't make sense, thinking people ignore them. You have laws against marijuana and gambling, for instance, which by their very existence on the law books create a network of smugglers, pushers, underground organized crime, and the like. In reality, some two hundred and fifty million of your people smoke marijuana regularly, and almost all of you gamble when the mood strikes, yet the presence of laws against these activities increases the prospect of illegal, evil conduct throughout all your cultures."

"Wouldn't legalizing gambling and marijuana be endorsing something that is not viewed by the majority as proper?" I asked.

"Do you want to talk about reality or fantasy?" she shot back. "Drug laws which protect the unknowing from charlatans and profiteers may serve a useful purpose. Education on the impact, side effects, and status of drug research would be necessary as a substitute to legislation. If in reality one third of the people do something, regardless of the laws against it, *that is what is,* and no amount of law enforcement is going to change it. If that's the case, then stop the wrong thinking. Be responsive to the wishes of the people. Clean it up. Use it as a revenue source. Keep it away from young children, and stop pretending that because you have passed a law against something and then proved you can't enforce it, you have done your job. In fact, you are hurting people by even bothering to have the law on the books in the first place. The fact that an activity is widespread in your culture means that it is endorsed. Whether you pass laws against it or not has nothing to do with reality. The people are still going to conduct themselves as they see fit, and your governments are simply going to involve a whole host of unsavory characters in the process of trying unsuccessfully to legislate morality and everyday behavior.''

"How do we get people into government who will be responsive to the wishes of the people?" I asked her.

"By changing the way you think, as well as the way you train people to think. Like everything else you've asked me, it boils down to your thinking. The people in government come from the same population that thinks *incorrectly*. There are very few risk takers in your population, very few honest, no-nonsense, reality-oriented people. Those you do have are usually ostracized and labeled as deviants. Your government representatives come from the general population and they impose the same wrong-way thinking in their tasks as lawmakers. You need people in government who are not afraid of losing their jobs—people who do not derive their personal value from their jobs, but from within. When people have a strong inner sense of value, they are never manipulated by fear of losing a job, since they know they can always move on and do virtually anything. You need people who see themselves as part of the *people* and who consequently would never enact a privileged set of laws for themselves and a less privileged set for everyone else. Once you begin the quality-minded and ethical re-thinking process, you will elect ethical people to work for you in your governments.''

She was obviously keenly aware of this issue and clearly saw the results of too much government and too few individual thinkers within the government. I don't think she would have been branded liberal or conservative.

When I asked her about these labels she laughed and commented, ''These are labels that critics need in order to compartmentalize and slot their representatives. I am a realist. I don't know what your labels mean. I despise your current welfare system, in which your government acts as if it were its own money that it dispenses. There is no such thing as welfare or government money in your reality. There are only individuals who are working, sending in money, and having it redistributed to people who do not work. If anyone does not work and is able, he ought to be required to pay back any money he receives while temporarily on welfare. Yet I also abhor the idea of the truly needy going without money. But the Earthly attitude appears to hold no objection to the truly needy receiving their share of the working people's money. They only object to entire generations of people who have chosen not to work expecting to be supported. Similarly, I feel that the concept of unemployment is something that governments have created so they will have an index. How can something called 'unemployment' exist when there are jobs going begging? A laid-off engineer who refuses to work as a sales clerk, which he is capable of doing, is not unemployed. He simply refuses to work. An attitude that something is owed to each person beyond the opportunity to take a risk, or that any work is superior, or inferior, is more wrong thinking. Your governments are made up of people who want to stay in power. They do everything they can to keep it that way, and you will continue to create unresponsive governments as long as you raise people who have to rely on power over others rather than their own inner sources of power over themselves to prove their worth.''

"Why are people willing to put up with this kind of treatment from lawmakers?" I asked.

"They aren't, except for short periods of time. In some places on your planet, you see people who have almost nothing living and working side by side with those who abuse them and exploit their labor for their own selfish ends. But this will not last. Your history has shown you this. Eventually the people rebel and start a revolution. On Earth, the disproportion between haves and have-nots is growing. Starvation on your planet is a government decision. It is a political fact, not a necessity as your government representatives in various parts of your planet would like the people to believe.

"People on Earth starve because it is accepted as normal, even with an abundance of food and the technology necessary to feed everyone. Governments allow it because they are consumed with power needs. Starvation is actually a tool they use to meet these needs. I saw tons and tons of food rotting on docks, while people starved only a few miles away on your planet. The reason, I learned in observing your government representatives around your globe, had to do with eligibility requirements, inspection regulations, paperwork, which prohibited the distribution of the food. This starvation was indeed a government decision. As the disproportion grows, the have-nots will stop accepting it. They will create revolutions that will force governments to be responsible to all people. They accept it now because they lack individual leaders who will lead the fight. But as those leaders materialize and surface, you will see dramatic shifts in power through force, unless you begin to elect, peacefully and purposefully, representatives to your governments who think realistically and *correctly*.''

"So you feel that our politicians, lawyers, and governments are generally afflicted with this same kind of 'incorrectness' in their thinking. They fail to see reality for what it is?" I asked, attempting to summarize.

"Yes, with the added bonus that the *power over others corruption factor* seems to be at work here. Your governments create massive military organizations which allow for absolutely no individual thought. In fact, they punish such thinking as a violation of the chain of command. Then these military units, with almost mind-boggling lethal capacities for destruction, are amassed and run by obedience-minded people who despise questions from anyone. Then you find yourselves fighting wars against your own people, wars that nobody wants. Your nonmilitary government functions are run with the same insensitive logic. You have individuals speaking about the need to economize who raise certain budgets when they get into office. They know what must be done, but their desire to stay in power permanently corrupts their thinking. The delusionary thinking of politicians continues unabated, and governments go on treating individuals as one big conglomerate which has no will or mind of its own. Until your governments begin to see those faceless masses as individual thinking people who will refuse, first as individuals, and then as masses, to continue sacrificing so that those in power may be kept more comfortably powerful, they will be looking directly into the mirror of their own demise. Your citizens will tolerate it, but only to a point.

"First you will see them lower their own taxes by passively refusing to pay, by surreptitiously going around the law. Then you'll see people ignoring the regulations and bypassing the governmental red tape that they depend upon for their very survival. Soon after, you will see a disregard for all laws, which at one time were only a few laws. This is how it breaks down. Only individuals with integrity, who think as the world *is*, rather than as they would like the world to be for their own personal advantage, can make your governments responsive to the individuals they are pledged to serve. But I didn't see any governments like that on your planet, and I looked earnestly."

"Is there any barometer we can use to see if we are headed in the direction you advise?" I asked.

"When there are no starving children on your planet, when there are enough day-care centers, when immunizations for all your children are readily available and fully funded, and when your governments have to conduct bake sales to raise money for their battleships and missiles, then and only then will you be in the place to which I refer. Speaking of bake sales, let's go to lunch,'' she said, informing me that she was putting an end to this portion of her gifts.

8 · Some Reality-
Only Reactions

This was to be our last afternoon together. Eykis
would be leaving the next morning. I knew she would
not change her mind. She was a woman of her word.
There was never any doubt about that. I was forced to
suspend my own feelings for her, and to get on with
her gifts to us. Returning to the recording studio, I
began the new tape.

"Eykis, you have discussed religion, business, education, medicine and government. You have described what you saw and what you feel might be done
to bring the messages and objectives of these disci-
plines into a new, beneficial alignment with reality
One major theme seems to emerge from your observations. We on Earth have a proclivity for thinking
incorrectly, as you put it, and for placing far too much
emphasis on external rather than internal processing.
Is this a correct summary?" I asked.

"Quite correct," she responded without hesitation.

Continuing this thought, she added, "You have become a people obsessed with thinking for each other, which is a polite way of saying, manipulating each other. Your governments want to think for their constituents, to regulate their lives, as if they couldn't make healthy decisions on their own. Your doctors insist that they are the only experts and classify anyone else who might lay claim to healthy thinking as an unqualified interloper. Your businesspeople feel that money is the source of happiness, and view inner happiness as the purview of hippies or unrealistic eggheads. Your educators insist that they know what others need, and they pursue external acquisitions rather than knowledge. Your religious leaders impose 'God's will' on others, always assuming that God is an external to be reached, rather than an inner concept to be experienced. The representatives from all five of your areas believe that they know what is best for others, and they spend their energy trying to impose what they know on those whom they serve. But your reality denies them the opportunity to do what they think they are doing. Thus they live an illusion and this illusion requires them to invent a thinking process to fit the illusion," she said.

"Well, in lieu of wearing additional hats this afternoon," I said, "I would like to give you some things to simply comment on, and then close with the ideas that you feel we most need. Is that acceptable?"

"I will be myself in any format of your liking," she replied laconically.

"All right, back to your illusions statement about the five topics. Precisely what is the illusion per se?"

"The illusion is that people do not possess free will and therefore can believe only what they are taught by means of others' teaching, proselytizing, governing, healing, or motivating. People on your planet are choosers, yet the leaders think they can choose for the people, and it simply isn't that way. That is the illusion. The road to enlightenment or self-awareness is an inner path. Leaders can only provide a healthy environment in which people can attain their own truths," she said.

"Then specifically, what is the thinking process that these 'leaders' invent, to support their illusions?" I asked, wanting to be deliberate and orderly for those who choose to think in these ways.

"The incorrect or illusional thinking process goes like this. Since I am an expert, I must know what is best for everyone. Therefore I will force-feed them what I know, and they will benefit from it," she said.

"And what would be a nonillusional thinking process for experts in any field?" I asked, continuing the systematic line of questioning to a conclusion.

"On Earth, people have unique minds. Since each person is different, one can never create policies, rules, or procedures that apply to all. The concept of 'everyone' simply does not exist. And on your planet too, your free-choice minds allow you to decide to learn or not learn, to know or not know, to obey or disobey, at any moment. You can change your free-choice minds an unlimited number of times on one issue or in any one moment. You are an ever changing, free-willed people. Correct thinking would acknowledge this fact and say: Each person must decide for himself what he wants each day. As a leader, I will expose you to the options and the likely consequences of these options. I'll even share my opinion if asked, but I'll never confuse it with *the* opinion, which simply doesn't exist. Since the road to enlightenment is an inner path, I won't insist that individuals pay me a toll for using their own road. It is their road and I'll help them travel it as they choose, as long as they don't attempt to exact tolls from others who desire to traverse their own highways. That would be 'correct' or nonillusional thinking, and that is what I addressed to the five representative issues you presented this morning,'' she concluded.

I decided to shift gears. It was obvious to me that this inner-versus-outer-thinking dilemma was a part of virtually all of our Earthly undertakings. If I engaged Eykis as General, Attorney, Florist, or Mechanic, the logic would still be the same. Her reality-only thinking always pointed to the illusional folly that she had just elaborated.

''I would like to have you comment briefly on several areas of interest to all human beings,'' I began. ''What do you feel about *parenting* as it is practiced here?''

''Here on Earth, I noted a strong desire of parents to believe that they own their children. The illusion is obvious. No one can own anyone else when everyone possesses free will. Remember, children have minds of their own too. Parents somehow have come to believe that their children owe them something just for being parents. You see children in a family being coerced into having the same religion, ethnic beliefs and prejudices, educational objectives, and the like. Parents somehow believe that membership in a family precludes thinking as an individual. They are surprised when young people want to be unique. They are often upset when their offspring want to marry outside of their own kind (whatever that is). They attempt to regulate, teach, and condition their children's thinking, and it doesn't work. The parents know it doesn't work, yet they carry on the battle and are forever upset and frustrated. It seems to me that the business of parenting ought to be to teach young people to be their own parents. Forget this business of family and parental obligations. Parenthood means raising children to think for themselves, by providing examples worth emulating. I would ask all parents to think back to how much they resisted, and still do, being owned by their own parents. I would also tell them to place their parenting emphasis on quality, ethics, integrity, knowledge, and serenity, and not the opposites, which I've discussed already."

"And what do you see as the role of discipline?" I asked her.

"The only worthy discipline is self-discipline. It is the ability to discipline oneself for full self-awareness and self-expression. Early in life a child needs a firm model to provide an environment in which to learn to internalize behavior, which is conducive to healthy self-management. The child needs to experience what will and will not be tolerated. All discipline of young children should be aimed at teaching self-discipline. If children learn only because they are told to do something, they soon become 'doing-as-they're-told' people. This is simply programming for incorrect thinkers and unfulfilled adults. In other words, parents need to model for them, and encourage them to discipline themselves, so that they have no need to rely on others for control.''

''What have you observed about marriage as it is practiced here?'' I asked Eykis.

''Marriage seems to be almost identical to parenting. It is invaded by the same incorrect thinking. That is why so many marriages end. You seem so determined in your quest for ownership that you even pursue it with your spouses. People who marry begin to think for each other. They impose expectations on each other, and this is intolerable to both partners because you are blessed with free will. Being an emotional or thought servant to another will be accepted for only a brief period of time here on Earth. Then the person who feels buried by the partner's 'thinking for two' simply refuses to continue and the relationship breaks down. In marriages that work, there is no incorrect thinking, no false assumption that one person has a right to think for another. As you know, on Uranus we have a reason for such behavior with our dependency-diodes and the like. That is our reality. But here you have no reality-based reasons for such conduct, and when dependency thinking surfaces, even in small doses, your marriages end, and remember, a marriage can end with or without divorce. Clean up the erroneous thinking and you will preserve your institution of marriage. Perpetuate it, and marriage will eventually disappear on your planet.''

"Do you think there is any such thing as *truth* here on Earth?" I wanted to know.

"There are unlimited truths on your planet, and they are all located in individuals. If you ask thirty people on the beach why this is a beautiful day, or is it too hot, you will get thirty different *truthful* answers. One will feel the day is beautiful because the sun is shining and it's warm, another will feel that it is a terrible day because of the same conditions. Both are truthful answers. On Earth, truth is an inner experience, yet many attempt to impose their truths on others without ever stopping to think about separate truths. Each person has an opportunity to view his world as he chooses. What is true for one is not true for another. When you allow for separate truths, you no longer need agreements about what is true. In fact, it is only when you attempt to organize a truth that it becomes a lie. Very few of the people on Earth whom I've observed are willing to accept another's truths as valid when they conflict with their own, or with the accepted 'organization' of a truth."

"You've mentioned changing our thinking as if it were something easy to do. How does one just change one's thinking?" I asked.

"You simply do it. For example, if I ask you to close your eyes and think of a brown cocker-spaniel puppy on a blue chair, you can do that. Then if I ask you to send that thought away and replace it with the thought of a green vase of twelve long-stemmed red roses, you could also do that. Can you tell me how you did it? Of course no one can say how it's done, but you all know how to change your thoughts. Forget the how and do it. Work at sending away any thought that you don't want or that is incorrect. This is the beauty of your reality, you can think as you choose.''

"What are your thoughts on psychiatry and psychology as they are practiced here?" I asked.

"Most of it is practiced by people who are trapped by the same incorrect thinking as those who seek the treatment. Most of your therapists (I thought that word was 'the rapist' the first time I encountered it) seem content to provide their clients with excuses for their own self-inflicted maladies. Your reality gives you a free will for a lifetime, yet you have professionals who convince their clients and each other of various theories which place blame on everything from the unconscious to birth order, to childhood traumas, to parental errors, or anything else that's convenient. Therapy seems to be an attempt by people to 'purchase friendship,' and an effort to gain self-understanding by looking backward. A person who practices this incorrect thinking of blaming others for his problems is simply transferring that blame when he looks to a therapist for the answers. The truly skilled therapists whom I observed provided an environment for self-discovery. They helped individual clients assume responsibility for everything and accept the fact that they alone were responsible for everything that happened to them. These were rare therapists, largely because you must believe this about yourself and be living this philosophy each day in order to help others to do the same. Only a knower of self can help a seeker of self to find self-knowledge.

And psychology, like all other professions, has few knowers of self, since its practitioners come from the same externally thinking population pool into which other professions dip as well."

There was so much to ask and yet I knew that whether we spent another day or a hundred years together, I would always feel that way. She would answer any question, discuss any subject, and she always revealed the depth of her reality-only thinking. I wanted to ask her how she felt about me, though I almost trembled at the thought of hearing someone talk to me, about me, without the ability to be even mildly dishonest. I wanted to know what she thought of Earthly love and sex, but again I decided to wait. I tried thinking as "correctly" as I knew how, and everything I felt for her said, "I love her." Yet I still doubted myself. How does one love someone who can only say and feel what is? What about the little white lies, or the occasional exaggeration to smooth things over?

I began to see myself in a new light. Was I afraid of her? Or was I afraid of myself? Since meeting Eykis I'd learned much about fear. When you elect to avoid anything because of fear, you choose to avoid life itself. Fear is a thinking process and it is based on believing that things are fearsome. But in reality, in Eykis' special reality, things on Earth just are. People don't possess little fear bugs as they might on Uranus. I was still afraid of being rejected by Eykis, but I was moving toward that inner road that she had defined earlier in the day. I wanted to take the time for myself.

I knew that she had more gifts to give. Still, I was going to ask her to share her unique knowledge and just present her secrets of the universe, without any interference from anyone, including myself. Then, perhaps, I'd ask how she felt about me. If there was time.

9 · The Secrets of the Universe

"You mentioned something about secrets in our earlier discussions, Eykis. Do you want these secrets to remain clouded over, or are you willing to share them here on film with us?" I asked.

"I'd be happy to share my observations with you. But first I would like to say that the only reason I refer to what follows as 'secrets' is that they appear to have eluded so many of you here on Earth. Originally I called them secrets because I thought no one knew them. I've since discovered that all these so-called secrets are available to everyone on Earth, and have been as long as you've had recorded history. I will still refer to them as secrets, however, because their actual use continues to remain obscure," she said.

"Fine. If you have no objections, I'm going to sit back and let you tell us, uninterrupted, what these universal secrets are," I replied, knowing full well that Eykis had no objections to anything I asked, since this was my format and she was the willing participant in this day-long encounter that was drawing to an end.

Eykis began . . .

"You must first *learn to cultivate your own garden.* I've noticed that most of your problems, your difficulties, your pain, and your self-defeating behaviors stem from ignoring this clearly necessary advice. Cultivating your own garden means that, as individuals, you focus first on the only thing over which you have absolute control, yourselves. Then, when you have your own life in order, you can assist others who need and seek your help. Your reality prohibits you from being anyone else, yet all of you seem to look critically into everyone else's gardens. Since all of you have the free will to grow what you please, it is really senseless to be concerned about what others grow in their gardens, unless they are interfering with someone else's right to self-determination. If your neighbors prefer green beans to your squash, then so be it. If your children choose to fertilize and you opt for crop rotation, then let it alone. If your spouse wants to grow flowers and leave the weeds where they sprout, and you prefer neat rows of alternate-colored vegetables, then that is how you ought to arrange your separate gardens. If you get your own garden in shape, growing what you choose, by methods that appeal to you, you will be so busy being and living that you won't have any time left over to criticize your neighbors' gardens. You will have time to admire and accept what they have created, and to assist those who ask your help or to help insure that no one grows crops that interfere in any way with the right of others to tend their own gardens.

Cultivating your own garden means accepting others as perfect, not wanting to alter or edit those you love, and putting your life energy into being the happiest, most fulfilled and moral human being possible. After all, your reality prohibits you from entering the gardens of others. So why not align your thinking to your reality, regardless of how much you dislike how others manicure their gardens? Liking or not liking the activities and life styles of others will only upset you and ruin your relationships. Moreover, you must have your own life in order before you can help others or work constructively at changing your world for the better. If all Earth people would remember this little secret, unhappiness in most forms would soon be eliminated.

"*The kingdom of heaven is within.* This secret, which I discussed earlier, is basic to your survival, and yet most of your people ignore it. The wording has a religious orientation, but the concept is not limited to religion. It applies to all human beings and their behavior. As a people, you resist looking inward. You've allowed yourselves to become external in almost all your human activities. You constantly seek pills to eliminate pain, drugs to get high, approval to feel loved, money to achieve happiness, psychologists to cope with life, and on and on you go on this external merry-go-round. Yet your reality allows you the wonderful privilege of having all you'll ever want or need by looking inward. You teach external thinking in all walks of life. You discourage reliance on self and trust of your inner signals almost as if they were a plague. You chastise and punish those who think for themselves and refuse to conform. You ask people to think like the herd and imprison those who refuse.

"From what I've noted, happiness, fulfillment, and purpose in life are all inner concepts. If you don't have inner peace and serenity, you have nothing, and still you scorn those who ask you to look inward and banish those who do so as a way of life. This simple secret is overlooked on your planet in all phases of life. You should reexamine your resistance to this fact of your reality. The kingdom of heaven symbolizes the ultimate perfection. It is not a place to arrive, nor a reward for being a conformist. It is within you to have this wonderful effortless perfection. It is yours for the taking. Looking inward will bring about serenity in all its luxurious forms on your planet.

"*Everything in the universe is exactly as it should be*. I've noticed that most of you on Earth absolutely refuse to accept what is, and instead opt for using up the precious currency of your lives, your present moments, in judging what is, and then choosing to be upset because you dislike your own judgments. You need to learn to look at the universe and say to yourselves, 'This is what I get. I'll accept it and enjoy it as it is. I'll work at changing what I dislike, and then tha will be what is. I'll refuse to become immobilized b, anything I encounter.'

"What you often forget is that everything and everyone on your planet exists as they are, independent of your opinions. You must learn to transcend judgment if you want to be happy. I've noticed that your older people judge the young, who judge them right back. Your whites judge your blacks and vice versa. Your males judge your females and females judge in turn. It is a large thinking sickness, since judgments begin with your minds. Instead of walking through life being mad at what is and what people choose to be, you might consider acceptance as an alternative. Instead of wishing that your reality were different, you might try treating it as a miracle worthy of being cherished. Freeing yourself of judgments would give you those moments you previously spent in judging for enjoying and being happy, and for working to improve what you dislike. True inner security will always elude those who sit in judgment, since they use up their life energy in anger at what is. You must first accept people and things for precisely what they are, before you can help to bring about positive change.

"Unfortunately, most humans see the world as they are themselves and therefore are almost always disappointed when the world fails to measure up to what they would like it to be. Your highest functioning people understand this secret. They use their common sense to accept what they can't change, their strength to tackle what they can change, and their wisdom to always know the difference. But first and foremost, they learn to accept everything and everyone in the universe as being exactly as they should be.

"*I hear: I forget. I see: I remember. I do: I understand.* This simple little secret seems to me to be ignored by most of you here on Earth. Your unique reality system prohibits you from understanding without internalizing and experiencing. No one on your planet can understand swimming, bicycle riding, dancing, making love, or anything else, without experiencing it. Yet you spend much of your energy on lecturing others, explaining endlessly how to do something, showing pictures and even telling each other how easy it was for ME to learn. Your educators provide far more 'hearing' and 'seeing' activities than 'doing' experiences, and then wonder why students understand so little. Earthly parents constantly criticize their children. They tell them how to think, how to feel, and how to behave, and then wonder why they are misunderstood. Your older people want your younger people to benefit from their experiences and so they lecture away, never seeming to grasp this basic secret. Individuals must experience their own reality their own way in order to understand. No one, regardless of how much he wishes it, can put understanding into another human being. Understanding can come only from doing, and on Earth, in sharp contrast to Uranus no one can provide understanding for anyone else.

" '*If one advances confidently in the direction of his dreams, and endeavors to live the life which he has imagined, he will meet with a success unexpected in common hours.*' This is a direct quotation from Henry David Thoreau, one of your own well-known philosophers. I include it as one of the secrets, because no one seems to understand it. Chasing success is like trying to squeeze a handful of water. The tighter you squeeze, the less water you get. With success, when you chase it, your life becomes the chase, and you never arrive at a place called successful. You become the victim of wanting more. I've noted that when you lead your lives in such a way that you personally feel fulfilled, doing what makes sense and feels right for you as a person, success will chase after you.

"One of the great ironies of Earth life seems to be that those who don't become consumed with chasing anything, including love, money, possessions, and approval, are the only ones who get these things in amounts sufficient to meet their needs. Those who don't care about being approved receive the most approval. Those who refuse to chase love seem to have plenty of it in their lives. Those who chase money may have enough of it, but they don't believe it, so they are still inwardly poverty-stricken. You can have success if you make it an inner rather than an outer process, and begin directing your energies toward living a fulfilled life.

"*Life itself is miraculous, therefore you need never seek miracles.* Everything in your life is a miracle to be cherished. A grain of sand, a bee on a flower, a sailboat, a cup of coffee, a wet diaper, a caterpillar, are all miracles. Those who see life as a miracle don't have time for despair or self-pity. When you learn to view life and everything in it as a miracle, you soon see that complaining is a waste of the miracle that you are. A complainer seldom stops to consider the alternative to his problems, which is, *having no life.* Life presents itself to you and asks nothing of you. You can take life and swim deliriously through it, or you can fight it. But when you elect to spend your time fighting it, you can't use the same time to enjoy it. Too many of you fail to appreciate what a gift life is. You bemoan your fate instead of realizing what a miracle t is that you are even here in the first place. You spend your time seeking miracles anywhere, from anyone, instead of seeing everything and everyone as a miracle in and of itself. When you cultivate a sense of appreciation for just being alive, you will have no time left for carping about this or that injustice. You will love life rather than fight it.

"*It's never too late to have a happy childhood.* So many of your people spend inordinate amounts of time complaining about their childhood experiences and blaming them for their empty adult lives. Since you don't have the benefits of rewind and re-do as we do on Uranus, it is literally a waste of your precious present moments.

"This too appears in my catalogue of 'secrets' because Earthlings don't seem to realize that they can have anything they missed as a child by simply opting to get it now. If you felt ignored as a child, then seek attention now. If you weren't allowed to ride a bicycle, or go to the amusement park, or dance, why not have the experiences today and leave the whining and blame behind? I've been perplexed by all this 'poor me' talk about childhoods here on Earth, since the remedy is so apparent. Since you can't go backward, complaining about the past will only make the present more unpleasant. And why choose to be miserable, when you can have whatever you missed out on . . . NOW!

"*Relationships that work, work because there is no work.* All of you spend so much of your precious life moments analyzing your relationships to death, literally to death. You want to talk about why you are happy or unhappy, what you like and dislike, where you are heading in your relationships, and so on. Talking about the relationship seems to be your way of covering up the fact that it isn't working. There is really only one sure way to make your relationships work, and that is to recognize each other's right to be separate, unique human beings without any 'ownership' expectations from each other. I have observed that the relationships in which this simple principle was respected by both people flourished. In relationships that ignored it, I noted constant haranguing, endless dull conversations, and ultimately a breakup. Relationships do not require work, they cry for and demand nothing more than mutual respect.

"*This is my way: What is your way? The way doesn't exist.* Another of your famous philosophers gave you this secret, which is almost universally ignored. Virtually everyone in a position of authority forgets this simple little secret. If you would stop trying to impose your way on others, and begin listening to what they might offer as alternatives, you could eliminate all your battles, from family fights to world wars. More listening and less demanding would eliminate the need to be right. Your separate beliefs that there is only one *right way* is, of course, an error, since there is no 'right' way. Once you stop trying to prove that you're right, you will eliminate the reactions that your wrong thinking engenders. A corollary of this secret is that *nobody likes being told what to do.* When you tell a child, a co-worker, a spouse, or a stranger what to do, that other person will almost always rebel and do something to the contrary. You all see this, yet you still continue *telling*, even though it rarely works. Being told what to do violates one's free will. It is an insult to the free thinking that is such a vital part of your reality. Stop trying to show people the right way, and begin asking about their way. You might just learn something, and you'll be helping to eliminate the hostility that always accompanies being told what to do.

"*You get treated in life the way you teach people to treat you.* You have no reason to blame anyone for how you are treated, and yet most of you think that the problems you face and the treatment you receive is the result of other people's lack of consideration. You have the inherent power to teach anyone how you want to be treated. When you simply sit back and accept being abused, you are responsible for permitting that abuse to be heaped on you. This is one of the 'secrets' because most of you seem to feel that other people cause your problems, hurt your feelings. I've noted that those people who refuse to be abused, insist on respectful treatment, and react swiftly and firmly when they are mistreated receive the respect that so many 'blamers' never see in their lives. Again, self-responsibility for all of your life experiences, rather than blame, is the key to a full, happy life. Teach those around you through behavior, not empty arguments, that you will tolerate nothing less than respect. This is never difficult for those who have self-respect, since a person with high self-esteem expects the same kind of treatment from others that they expect of themselves. Respect yourself, and you'll receive respect. If you receive disrespect, look to yourself and ask that most important question, 'Why have I allowed myself to be treated this way?' instead of, 'Why are they doing this to me again?'

"*Wherever I go, there I am!* You cannot escape yourself. On Earth you cannot run away to a distant place and solve your problems. The cause of your difficulties is within yourself. *You must get you* straightened out first, then it won't matter where you are. I've seen people take refuge in liquor but they still have to face themselves. I've seen people try to escape problems in exotic vacation lands, and still the problems persist. You can change marriage partners and repeat the same patterns of ownership and mutual disrespect. You Earthlings fail to see your problems as internal. Thus you make every attempt to run away from them. But it never works. Thus I include this in the itemization of 'secrets.' You just don't seem to be aware of your inability to run away from difficulties and problems. Anything that bothers you is a problem only within. Your world doesn't care about it, nor do the people in it. Only you experience it and only you can correct it. Running away only provides you with a new setting to experience the same old inner churning. On Earth, 'Wherever I go, there I am' is indeed worth remembering.

"*Keep it simple*. You want to make life complicated. You endorse big fancy words that no one understands over simple language and call it intelligence. You use mumbo-jumbo in your legal systems, your contracts, insurance policies, tax laws, mortgages, and on and on. Then you hire 'experts' to wade through the mazes you've created. In religion, philosophy, psychology, medicine, law, education, economics, and almost every form of human enterprise, you attempt to keep things complicated and somehow maintain that simplicity means simple-minded. Yet your best writers, composers, artists, and educators are those who use clear, precise language and style to convey their meaning.

"None of you wants anything you touch to be fuzzy and complicated, yet all of you seem to strive for more befuddlement as a way of showing that you have arrived at a higher plateau than your neighbors. You give status to those whom you can't understand, believing them to be more intelligent because they are more confusing. Keep it simple! This simple advice will help you to enjoy your lives. You humans are not really that complex, and enjoying life is quite a simple matter, if you eliminate the confusion and just do it. The more obtuse you make your language, the more confusing you make your policies, the more you lose sight of the simple beauty of being alive. If you want to accomplish anything on Earth, the best advice is to do it, as opposed to making it a hugely difficult mental process.

"*These are the good old days*. So many of you are tied up in the senseless frenzy of pursuing the future and reliving the past. Your thinking becomes so clouded that it erodes the present moment, which is all you have on Earth. *Now* seems to be scorned in favor of planning. You reward 'futurizing'—planning ahead, saving for your old age, and postponement of gratification—while punishing those who live fully with such labels as irresponsible and hedonistic. You are constantly in the unreal position of never living fully today. I say unreal because it is impossible for you here to live in any moment other than this one, yet you elect to expend your present moments futurizing and reliving, while deluding yourselves into thinking this is really happening. *Now is it!* You have no rewind and no fast-forward on Earth. When you begin to use up your present moments living them, instead of reliving or planning for a future moment in which you can relive them, you will have a hold on living in the only possibility that your reality allows, NOW.

"*You are perfect*. For some reason you've chosen to believe that perfection is anathema in people, and consequently you are doomed to a lifetime of striving for something you can never attain. You've confused being perfect with being flawless, and cannot see the perfection of yourselves as constantly changing beings. You feel that it is somehow imperfect to be perfect. Most of you know that all of nature is perfect. Your roses and sunsets are perfect. You allow for your pets, trees, and mountain ranges to be perfect, and yet when it comes to your most magnificent creations—your people—your assignment for them is to be perpetually striving, but never arriving. You're perfect! Of course you are ever changing. Certainly you can grow and evolve. But you are still perfect creations who can be fulfilled only when you stop seeing yourselves as always having to deny your full perfection. Your lives are never finished and completed the way you think they ought to be. When you die, you all have half-empty bottles of shampoo, and some canned food left in the cupboard. You are given a limited amount of time to live, and while you are doing it, you might like to know that everything on your planet that is natural is also perfect. Your life is here for a while. It constantly changes shape, form, and even substance, and all of it is perfect even if you decide to call it by another name, such as imperfect.

"*There is no way to happiness: happiness is the way!* This is the message of all my gifts. If you haven't figured out this secret, happiness will always elude you.

"These are my so-called secrets," Eykis said. "Use them as you see fit. They are based on firsthand observations by an outsider—a unique outsider, in that I must operate from a 'what-is' reality. You all have such an advantage here on Earth: Your reality permits you to live in total harmony with your world. Yet up to now you've chosen disharmony at almost every turn. Why not take these gifts, apply them, and just attempt to experience a new reality?" she concluded.

I was stunned by her ability to state her observations with such clarity. But I didn't want the day to end. I had one more selfish task to attend to before she left.

"I haven't asked you about love yet," I said, adding, "As you are no doubt aware, this is a subject that has been written about by authors, poets, composers, and artists of all stripes since we've had people on our planet. You haven't addressed yourself to this specific subject, even though you've touched on it in your gifts to us today," I said.

"You're asking me about this now because you believe that you are in love with me and you're afraid of my leaving you. Isn't that correct?" she asked.

"Yes, that is true, and much, much more. I've loved you since the first moment I saw you on that television screen. It is a unique love for me. It has nothing to do with your appearance; in fact as I dozed off to sleep last night, I was thinking of you and I couldn't for the life of me remember what you looked like. I am, for the only time in my life, in love with a being rather than a body. With a soul instead of an appearance. I've wrestled with your leaving me today, and while I want to be noble and strong, I must confess that the thought of your disappearing from my life is painful. I need to know how you see this love, your feelings for me, and then perhaps the inner torture that I know I'll experience when I must face life without you will ease," I concluded.

"You speak of love like most people here. Somehow you've convinced yourself that love itself requires the object of your love to be in your presence for you to be fulfilled. Again, 'incorrect thinking' takes over for you. By your definition of love, you can *never* be happy in love. Your love is an 'I need you here' love. It requires me, or someone, or even something, external to yourself to satisfy your love desires. But love isn't really like that here on Earth from what I've learned. Love, too, is an inner concept. It is located within you. It is yours to experience for whomever or whatever you choose. It requires no reciprocity. Indeed, when you ask for anything in return, you no longer have love. You have then sullied it with expectations and demands, no matter how slight they may be.

"It is precisely because of these expectations that there is so little genuine love on your planet. Most of you are jealous and possessive in your love. When your love turns to possessiveness it makes demands. The demands then alienate the loved one and you incorporate anger and fear into the relationship. With these come bitterness and aggression, and whether we speak of individual love relationships or global interactions, what you call love, but is in fact ownership and manipulation, takes over and the problems to which I've addressed myself today then flow," she stated.

"But can we really have love without expectations? Certainly people want their love returned, otherwise it would be a one-way proposition," I countered.

"Your love is located within you. It is yours to nurture and savor, to give to others in any way you choose. This is true for others as well. If someone you love fails to return the love the way you would like it returned, that is the other person's choice. It doesn't at all detract from your love. While you may wish that your love were reciprocated, to insist upon reciprocation is to place your ability to love in the hands of others. This notion, while difficult for you to accept, is the very foundation of love. Love must be without qualifications or demands. I know you would like me to say something quite different right now, but your love must not depend on being loved. You must learn to find ecstasy in other people's happiness. You must ask nothing of your love. In fact, love as I define it can be experienced only by those who know themselves and have no fear of a detached love. Once you feel love for yourself, it is quite normal to give it away. And giving it away without any expectations can lead to a resolution of most of your Earthly problems. With no expectations, you will find it quite easy to love those who refuse to love you. In fact, you will stop looking for antagonisms and enemies and will give love instead. Love is your perfection. Every one of you wants love. Few of you know that *love for yourself* provides you with the ability to love others, that only a person who experiences love within is capable of genuine detached love," she stated.

"You mean that a person who loves others by your definition of detached nonexpectations is someone who loves himself first? Isn't that a selfish and conceited kind of love?" I wondered.

"It's quite simple, my friend. You can't give away what you don't have. Those who love, love without qualification. They love their assigned enemies and those who would do them what you call "harm," and if everyone learned to love in this way, there would be no assigned enemies, and people would practice a kind of love heretofore limited to only a few of you here on Earth. Love is really the solution, but only when it's used in the sense I've just described. The true test of love is loving those who refuse to return it as you would prefer," she said.

"I assume that this too means that you'll be leaving me here, and that if my love is genuine, it will be within me and that will be enough?" I asked.

"How could anything you feel be anywhere but within you?" she asked right back.

"It can't, but it would be nicer for me if you stayed here and shared that love as well," I countered.

"But that wouldn't be love you're talking about. It might indeed be nicer, but it would still need my presence here in order for you to love, and that is at the core of all that 'incorrect thinking' I've been talking about since we first met two weeks ago."

"Then you must go," I said solemnly.

"In reality, I am going at this moment by way of molecular transport."

"But wait! One more thing. What can I say to people who feel empty, as I do now, when things don't go as they would like them to go? To those who feel trapped as I do now, by the circumstances of their lives? To those who feel cheated? I can't just say, 'Think correctly.' They would laugh at me. They really believe they are thinking properly. They believe their problems are real and don't feel that they can send them away by just changing their thinking and attitudes." I was talking faster, hoping for a reprieve. I knew the inevitable was upon me. Eykis was on her way. I just didn't want to muster up the inner courage to say farewell in a noble way. I still wanted to hang on, but I knew it was useless, and I knew that she was correct.

"Well, what do I tell them, and myself as well?" I almost begged.

Her voice and form begin to fade. "Were you not called the Learner? The lessons are complete, and you can celebrate your graduation by accepting my gifts and assuming your new role. In reality, the gifts I gave you were always yours. I merely unwrapped them and revealed them to you. Did you not notice the shining container? The gifts were enclosed in my love. You have that, too, my friend. Now give *your* gifts, Teacher. Your world of learners awaits you . . .''

EPILOGUE

Inspired, I determined not to let any time slip by before I made the world aware of the gifts from Eykis. My contacts with the television industry and other international media were minimal, so my approaches to them were futile. Producers in charge of programing said the tapes were obviously a fake, or at least a sci-fi docudrama which could not be aired without being censored, edited, rewritten. The more adamant I became, the more they looked upon me as a mad scientist, too close to the edge for comfort, too great a risk as far as advertisers were concerned. I refused to be defeated.

Back at the campus, my student days were over, but I had become an assistant professor in physics and biochemistry. This gave me access to the laboratories and libraries where I had studied the *Urantian Formulas*. Although my initial work, and the successful experimental flight to Uranus, had been secret, the teaching position provided a public audience for the ideas of Eykis and the basic concepts of molecular transport. It would have to do. If I could not begin on the broad base that Eykis had imagined would be available (as it would have been on Uranus), at least I could begin with the fertile open minds of young men and women in pursuit of knowledge in pure science. I lived the *reality-only* gifts I had been given. Let them learn from a role model. And I taught what they would need as a basis for understanding the molecular-transport equations.

After several years during which I published articles in physics journals on the most rudimentary preliminaries, there began to be excitement about my work. Students who had no intention of specializing in science enrolled in my classes just to hear the "common sense" that came through in my lectures. I was annually chosen the most popular teacher at the university. My lectures filled the largest auditorium. Complaints abounded from my colleagues because I was "not teaching physics but running a sideshow." The dean of the college firmly reminded me that I was not to have so many uninvited guests in my classrooms, since they were depriving the paying students of parking spaces in the student parking lots. However, the department chairman, who was seeking a way to get rid of me, was told in no uncertain terms that I was not to be interfered with, since I was single-handedly keeping the physics department alive by luring students into my classes.

I knew I was popular with the young people, but I didn't want them to follow my lead like groupies or cult worshipers. I wanted them to understand how I had first learned about reality and then simply decided to live in it. Because of my reputation on campus, I persuaded the manager of the campus cinema, a student-operated business that showed movie classics, to present my tapes of Eykis.

There was very little advance publicity, but many of my students and their friends attended. I expected them to be skeptical, as the media professionals had been, but kinder because of their regard for me.

As the tapes were shown I became oblivious to the audience. My eyes streamed with tears as I saw her beauty and nobility again. She was alive and as lovely as ever. Her truth beamed down like sunlight between the gray cloud of Earthly pettiness and neuroses. It was painful to see the tapes ending, but as I had lived their creation, I was prepared for their final moments. I was not prepared for the audience reaction.

First there was silence. Not a calm stillness, but the electric, utter silence before the storm. Then, like a human cyclone, the audience began to rise and roar, clapping, shouting, whistling, shaking each other, laughing, screaming, weeping, jumping on the rattling folding chairs, tearing their programs to confetti. Gradually a chant for the "author" began. I stepped forward, simply to calm them.

In seconds the students raised me on their shoulders and carried me around the theater like a hero. I was stunned, but joyous that Eykis had been welcomed at last. To clear the building the manager said the tape show would be repeated the following evening, but only if the patrons left the place immediately. We left, but could not disband. A large crowd descended on the nearby pizza shop. Filled to capacity, the place throbbed with the quickened beat of debate and delight. Every table was the scene of young people arguing about the meaning, the impact, the clarity of the film. I couldn't sit still for any one conversation. I zigzagged about the restaurant drinking in the scene, devouring the triumph of Eykis. Who needed beer and pizza!

Again and again I was asked, "Who is Eykis really? Is she from Hollywood? What accent was that? Would she come back for interviews?" No one accepted the most obvious—she was what she said she was—a Urantian.

The films were shown the following night to a packed house. While the tapes were playing, the manager tried to persuade me to allow copies of the tapes to be made and shown on other campuses through the intercollegiate film network. I saw an opportunity to reach a receptive audience on a wide scale, but I wanted to protect Eykis from misuse of the films. I told him he could continue presenting the films locally but the originals would remain with me after each showing. Until I had a copyright, there would be no exporting, and with a copyright, no exploiting. At the end of the second night's program the reaction was much the same—reverent silence exploding into wild delight or fierce denial. There were no neutral reactions in the house.

For several weeks the tapes were viewed by students and faculty. Word spread and students from other universities appeared on campus hoping to get in. Local newspapers reported the reaction of viewers and sent reporters to get the "real story" from me. Everyone wanted to meet the actress who had played the role of Eykis. No one believed my "foolish publicity stunt" of insisting that she could not be found on Earth.

Years before, just after my return from Uranus, I'd had several copies made of the *Urantian Formulas* and put them in safekeeping in various places, including my memory. I was glad they were not readily available, because not long after the Eykis tapes were duplicated and released for national campus distribution, both my apartment and my laboratory were ransacked. Someone was taking interplanetary travel very seriously. The police said that whatever the burglars were after was not found, so they very well might go after the source—me!

Most people, including the scientific community, regarded the tapes as science fiction as far as Eykis' role was concerned. I did not try to change their minds while the fear of kidnaping haunted me. But I continued my lectures in class and wrote more bits about the formulas, adding pieces to the puzzle to entice physicists all over the world to speculate in the correct direction.

In a remarkably short time there were tremendous changes. First on campus and then everywhere I went people were wearing buttons proclaiming, "Eykis lives!" or "I like Eyk!" There were pins with an enameled eye in the center circumscribed by the slogan, "Keep an Eye on Reality!" Bumper stickers announced "Happiness Is the Way" and "Keep It

Simple!'' A landscaping service advertised with a drawing of Eykis holding a bouquet: ''Cultivating your own garden? See us for ideas!'' An art student hung a banner over the campus chapel door, ''The kingdom of heaven is within. Please enter.'' I was afraid Eykis' message was being taken too lightly. Students were ''zapping'' imaginary lasers of guilt and hurt feelings by aiming their index fingers like pistols. Did they get the real message along with the amusement?

Our Earthly problems were serious and Eykis had been sincere. Was all this levity and casual quotation really the way to make an impact? Apparently yes. Over a matter of months the films became the source of much discussion. In schools, classes in psychology, sociology, medicine, religion, philosophy, political science, and business administration discussed the films. Politicians at all levels were seen wearing Eykis buttons and voting on legislation dealing with health care, defense budgets, education, and all the vital issues Eykis had discussed. Their consciousness was raised and their constituents were aware. Holistic medical clinics developed overnight. Corporations held seminars on how Eykis' ideas applied to business. Transcripts of the tapes were presented on stages across the country by the most talented performers. Ecumenical conclaves issued declarations of support for the philosophy.

While I gloried in the evidence of impact on the emotional, spiritual, and physical health of the people of my country, I was not really aware of how quickly the Eykis influence would spread. The films were subtitled in forty languages and distributed all over the world. Even where the tapes were censored, uncut copies were smuggled in, causing an uproar impossible to suppress. Then came the telegram: I had been awarded the Nobel Prize for physics for my research in molecular transport!

After much thought, I decided that the *Urantian Formulas* were a gift to the Earth, not to me, and that as the teacher, I must now convey the full knowledge of the Formulas as well as the gifts of Eykis. Eykis had wanted a worldwide audience initially, and I could not then provide it. Now, because of the burglary scare, I dared not draw international attention in any sensational way. But once the Formulas were shared, there would be no threat to them or me, and the solemn presentations of the Nobel Prizes would create the distinguished audience Eykis had sought.

In great happiness and haste, I asked for and received a week's leave from the university, prior to the Nobel ceremonies. My friends thought I traveled to Sweden, but my actual round trip was of considerably greater distance. However, I arrived in Stockholm on the proper day, thrilled to meet with the giants of the Earth in the civilized cordiality of that sparkling capital city.

That evening, the presentations were made in formal glory. The subdued elegance could not diminish the excitement. The atmosphere was a fine combination of proud self-esteem and deepest respect for the assembled masters. When it was my turn to receive my prize, my heart raced. The bright lights of glowing chandeliers and popping cameras blinded me, yet lit the path to the podium.

Before speaking, I breathed deeply.

I began: "The reward I accept for my work in physics is that tonight I may stand before you, the great of all nations, and walk among you, as a true friend. Yet the prize which you bestow cannot rightfully be mine alone, for the information was a gift from the masters of another world. Internationally, there are talented physicists and scientists of many fields who are close enough to the solution to the transport puzzle to enable me to feel safe in completing the missing segments. I have the *Urantian Formulas* with me tonight to distribute to you all. And I bring proof of their validity in the presence of the lady Eykis of whom many of you have heard.

"She left Uranus a short while ago and I must move over slightly so she can comfortably materialize on this platform. Ah! I feel her energy beside me. Eykis! Please come among us. Welcome to a better planet than you visited before!"

The shimmering flecks of her dancing molecules began to swirl beside me. I could hear the gasps of the audience.

I could see those smiling honest eyes again . . .